THE QUEST FOR RETIREMENT UTOPIA

How to Find the Retirement Spot
That's Right for You

By Dave Hughes

Prickly Pair Publishing
Chandler, Arizona, USA

Other retirement lifestyle books by Dave Hughes:
Design Your Dream Retirement: How to Envision, Plan For, and Enjoy the Best Retirement Possible
Smooth Sailing into Retirement: How to Navigate the Transition from Work to Leisure

Visit www.RetireFabulously.com to discover more valuable resources and informative articles about retirement lifestyle planning.

If you would like to contact the author, please send email to TQFRU-book@retirefabulously.com.

Editor: Debra Gaskill
Cover photo: Jan Alexander
Cover design: Dave Hughes

Portions of this content have previously appeared on my website, RetireFabulously.com and/or my blog on U.S. News.com.

Library of Congress Control Number: 2019920455

ISBN-13: 978-0-9970017-4-7
ISBN-10: 09970017-4-7

Table of Contents

Introduction...1

    Welcome!..3

    Why Do You Want to Move After You Retire? 7

What is Most Important to You? 13

    What's Really Important? 15

    Taking a Long-Term View 27

    Best Places to Retire Lists – Fact, Fiction, or Fantasy? 31

    The Great Data Crunch..35

    What to Look for When You Visit a Potential Retirement Destination 41

Best and Worst Places to Retire in the United States 45

    Where Can You Pay the Least Taxes?...47

    A Quick Look at Each State..53

        New England 55

        Mid-Atlantic 57

        Southeast..60

        Florida...66

        Midwest...67

        Great Plains 72

        South-Central..73

        Southwest 76

        Rocky Mountains...79

        Northwest..83

        California..86

        Hawaii...87

Is a 55+ Active Adult Community Right for You? 89

    The Retirement Community Phenomenon......................................91

    Changing Retirement Trends 95

    12 Factors You Must Consider Before Moving to a 55+ Retirement
    Community...103

    Sun City Revisited..111

Other Considerations 113

    The Case for Staying in Place 115

    Is Downsizing the Right Choice for You?.....................................119

    Should You Rent or Buy?..123

    Avoid These Common Mistakes When Choosing Where to Retire.......125

Alternative Retirements 129
    Retiring to a Rural Area 131
    Living in an RV 137
    Living on a Houseboat 147
    Living on a Cruise Ship 149
    World-Wide Nomadic Living 155
Retiring Overseas 157
    Why Retire Overseas? 159
    Can You Really Save Money by Retiring Overseas? Should You?.......161
    Where Can You Retire? 167
    The Value of Expat Communities 175
    Buying or Renting a Home in Another Country 179
    Accessing Healthcare 183
    Taxation and Other Financial Concerns 187
    Culture Shock 191
    Resources for Planning your International Retirement 201
    Retiring to Mexico 205
    Retiring to Central or South America 219
        Costa Rica 222
        Panama 224
        Ecuador 226
        Uruguay 228
        Chile 230
    Retiring to Europe 233
        Portugal 236
        Spain 240
        France 243
        Malta 245
    Retiring to Southeast Asia 251
    Retiring to New Zealand 253
LGBT Concerns 255
    Evaluating LGBT Resources and Friendliness 257
    Retirement Communities for LGBT Seniors 263
    Best US Cities for LGBT Retirees 269
    LGBT Laws and Rights Around the World 279
Conclusion 283
    Can Moving to the Right Place Really Make You Happier? 285
    Are You Ready to Embark Upon Your Quest? 287

PART ONE

Introduction

.

Chapter 1

Welcome!

If you could live anywhere in the world, where would you choose?

For now, assume that cost is not a factor and you could afford to live wherever you want.

Hopefully you have at least one place in mind, and maybe several.

Now for the bigger question: *Why?*

What characteristics of the place(s) you thought of seem so appealing to you?

It's fun to dream about where you want to retire. Once you no longer have your job tying you to a particular area, there's no reason not to relocate to a place that's more to your liking. Perhaps you want to move someplace warmer, closer to the water, or where the pace of life is slower.

You may be motivated to stretch your retirement dollars by moving to a place where the cost of living or the tax burden is lower. Healthcare costs are exorbitant in the United States and significantly cheaper elsewhere in the world.

But with so many factors to consider, choosing a place that's right for you can become overwhelming. With the help of this book, you will be better equipped to cut through the daunting and often conflicting information. You will be able to identify and focus on what's really important for you, which will help you identify places that are the best match for you.

The Internet and various magazines offer a wide range of lists of top places to retire. But contrary to what these lists try to tell you, there is no one perfect place to retire. If there was, millions of people would flock there. It would quickly become dense and overcrowded, and it would cease to be a desirable retirement destination.

My purpose is to help you four ways:

1. To help you clarify what is most important to you, and to suggest some considerations that you may not have thought of.
2. To suggest new possibilities for where – and how – you might retire. In other words, to help you think outside the box.
3. To dissuade you from making a poor choice for where to retire. At times, it will seem as though I'm dwelling a lot on the negative aspects of places, or that I'm playing devil's advocate and poking holes in all the places you thought you might want to live.

   I am.

   It's easy to think about places to live in idealized terms, and many websites and brochures accentuate only the positive. Choosing where to live is as much about avoiding the negative factors as it is about maximizing the positive ones. Often warts are hidden and you don't discover them until after you have moved.

4. To provide you with the resources you need to properly evaluate the places you are thinking about retiring, so that you can make the most informed choice – the choice that is right for you.

This book will prepare you with the facts and resources you need, the questions you should ask and get answered, and the factors you should consider as you embark upon your quest for *your* Retirement Utopia – the retirement destination that's right for you.

Throughout the book, I will mention many websites that are excellent resources. I'll offer a couple downloadable worksheets. All of those may be found online at RetireFabulously.com/quest-resources. I encourage you to bookmark that page and return to it periodically. I will do my best to update it with new information as it becomes available, add new websites as I discover them, and fix or remove broken links which inevitably happen from time to time.

Chapter 2

Why Do You Want to Move After You Retire?

There are many reasons why you might want to move after you retire. Some of them overlap, and more than one may apply to you.

Here are just a few:

1. Cheaper cost of living

Of course, we would all prefer to spend less money on living expenses. Even if you have saved adequately for retirement, you are probably facing the prospect of living on a fixed income that is not as high as what you have been accustomed to making.

But if your retirement savings fall considerably short, a move to a place with significantly cheaper cost of living may be a necessity.

Within the United States, the cost of living varies widely. There are many parts of the equation – it isn't just the cost to buy or rent a house and the price of groceries. Taxes differ significantly from state to state, and the total picture is a complex mix of income, property, sales, gasoline taxes, and more. Medical care costs differ from state to state, especially if you are younger than 65 and need to purchase your own insurance. Utility costs also vary widely, both by rate and by how much you will need to heat or cool your home in the climate you live in.

Certain countries in Central America, South America, and Southeast Asia have received a lot of attention as places where retirees could live for as little as $1,500 per month, including some money in the budget for eating out, Internet access, and entertainment. It's important to note that you will probably be living in a much smaller space and living much more simply in these places. Of course, that may be exactly what you want. In other words, the cheaper cost of living comes paired with a more basic, stripped-down lifestyle.

Healthcare is more expensive in the United States than almost anywhere else. One of the greatest drivers for moving to another country is cheaper healthcare. Lower cost does not necessarily equal lower quality; France, Malta, Portugal, and Spain, for example, have some of the best healthcare systems in the world,[1] at significantly lower costs. The quality of healthcare in most developed and developing countries is very good, and entirely adequate for most medical situations.

The low cost of living should never be the only reason you move somewhere. Unless you are forced to get by on just your Social Security check, it shouldn't even be the primary reason. You'll spend the rest of your life being miserable. You'll be spending less money while living in a place you hate.

2. Different climate

Generally, people who desire to live in a different climate choose to move someplace warmer, such as Florida or Arizona. Conversely, some people who live in hot climates may prefer to retire to someplace cooler.

Some retirees are migratory, moving to sunnier, warmer climates during winter. In Phoenix, some present and future retirees want to move to cooler climates during summer. This is an alluring option for many, but be sure to factor the cost of owning or renting a second home or maintaining a recreational vehicle (RV) into your retirement budget if you choose to do this.

---

[1] According to the World Health Organization's 2010 rankings of the healthcare systems of every country in the world. There has not been a worldwide ranking by a reputable source since 2010. http://thepatientfactor.com/canadian-health-care-information/world-health-organizations-ranking-of-the-worlds-health-systems/

3. Live in a place that's more to your liking

On a theoretical level, you always have the choice of where to live. On a practical level, where you live may be heavily influenced by where your job is or where good job opportunities exist. Once you retire, you are no longer bound by this constraint. There's nothing holding you to an area that you don't like or, to look at it more positively, there's nothing to stop you from living where you really want to live.

There are several factors that contribute to making a place likable, in addition to your preferred climate.

One is recreational amenities. If you play sports such as golf or tennis, you'll want to live someplace that has good golf courses and tennis courts. If you like boating, you'll want to be near water. If you plan to enjoy hiking and nature, you'll want to live someplace that offers those options.

Another is cultural amenities. If music, art, and theatre are important to you, you'll want to live someplace where you can attend performances or perhaps participate actively in those pursuits.

You may also be motivated to find a political or social environment where you will feel more comfortable. If factors such as gun violence, racism, religious intolerance, or homophobia are of concern to you, you may want to move someplace where the society is better aligned with your values and priorities.

Similarly, you may be deeply concerned about the direction the country is headed politically. Keep in mind that the political scene changes every few years as new presidents are elected and party control of Congress switches back and forth. This doesn't only apply to the United States. If you are thinking about moving to another country, expect that the political climate in that country may change, too.

4. Closer proximity to loved ones

You may want to live closer to aging parents, friends, or your children and grandchildren. For some people, this is the most important criterion.

5. A new adventure

This is often the most alluring and possibility-filled reason to move. After years of living in the same place, you may yearn to discover new lands and experience new cultures in a way that you just can't do on a brief vacation.

This may involve permanently moving to a new place (domestically or internationally), or it may mean a nomadic lifestyle in which you travel the country or the world in an RV, on a houseboat, or in a series of short-term rentals.

These are all great reasons to move after you retire.

As much as this book is filled with possibilities for what might be, and as much as it is fun to dream about living a carefree life in an ideal place, you should proceed very carefully after much thought and many conversations with your spouse (if you have one).

Simply put, the grass is not always greener on the other side.

As another old cliché goes, no matter where you go, there you are.

No place is perfect. No matter where you live, there will be some aspects of living there that are less than ideal. Some of the worst characteristics of a place may be the ones hidden farthest beneath the surface.

It's important to identify what your true motivations are. Doing this will help you define the factors that are most important to you and help you guard against getting swept away by a beautiful beach or some other idyllic setting that may seem perfect after a few days of vacation, but would present many drawbacks for permanent living.

I am perpetually curious about other places. Sometimes when I travel to other countries, I try to imagine what it might be like to live there. I research that place to learn more about the cost of living, social and political environment, immigration requirements, and so forth. Sooner or later, the disadvantages of living there become more apparent. Would I miss my friends? Would I have the same opportunities to play music or go to concerts and theatre? Would I have to learn a new language, and could I do that easily? Would I miss Costco? Ultimately, I always come to the conclusion that I'm probably best off right where I am now.

Even when I search other neighborhoods in my area for places where I could enjoy the same quality of life but with lower house prices, the answer is usually the same: I'm best off where I am now.

A human characteristic many of us share is that the thrill we get from anticipating something is often greater than the actual pleasure we derive from that thing once we have it.

That's why it is so important for you to become crystal clear on why you want to move and what your most important criteria are.

It may seem like I am placing a lot of importance on this – I am. Where you live in retirement may not be a life-or-death issue, but this decision carries more weight than it did for moves you made when you were younger. If you were offered a job or a transfer to a particular city, chances are you just moved there and found a good place to live that met your criteria for what you could afford, proximity to your job, and maybe a few other things. You probably didn't think too much about the cost of the move, because you knew you would continue to earn money during the coming years.

When you move after you retire, the cost of moving becomes more significant. Any money you spend on moving expenses, your realtor's commission, and fixing up your new home comes from your retirement savings, which are more likely to be finite. Multiple moves will result in multiple drains on your remaining money.

Plus, moving requires strength and effort. It's a hassle. The older you get, the less you will be able to tolerate the physical demands of moving. And if you are like most people, you have accumulated a vast inventory of possessions throughout your life that you will need to either move or get rid of. The days of accomplishing your move with a couple of pick-up trucks or a 12-foot rental van are long gone.

Chances are, any move you make during retirement may very well be your last move – at least until it's time to move into assisted living or a nursing home.

That's why it's so important to make this choice wisely. You may be able to afford to make this move and have the stamina for it, but if you end up somewhere you don't like, you might not have the resources and the strength for another move.

Before you continue farther into this book, take some time over the next few days to ponder the question, "Why do I really want to move?" Write your answers down.

Some answers may be obvious. If you know that your retirement savings have fallen short and you need to live as economically as possible, your overriding reason for moving after you retire would be to live cheaply and stretch your retirement savings further.

But if your reasons for wanting to move seem to be vague or idealized, you might want to spend some more time examining and clarifying your motivations. For example, if your reason for moving is that you dream of spending each day of your retirement relaxing on a tropical beach, sipping a Mai Tai, and listening to the gentle sound of the waves washing up on the beach, you may need to think about this some more. That would be fun for a few days, but it would get old quickly and you would become bored and miserable.

PART TWO

What is Most Important to You?

Chapter 3

What's Really Important?

When you first begin thinking about moving after retirement, your initial choice or choices may be based on surface-level appeal. For example, if you live in a cold, snowy region, Florida may seem like an obvious choice. If you have enjoyed wonderful vacations in Hawaii, you might set your sights on retiring there. A peaceful cabin in the mountains or on a lake might appeal to you.

These places seem appealing because they serve as a welcome change of scenery and pace from your day-to-day life. They provide an escape and a breath of fresh air. Unfortunately, most wonderful vacation spots make poor choices for permanent living.

A remote location may be peaceful and relaxing, but you could be far from shopping and good doctors and hospitals, your entertainment options might be limited, and options for socialization will be fewer.

In popular tourist spots, the tourists and the traffic they bring will become annoying. The businesses and attractions that cater to the tourists will become places you prefer to steer clear of. And once you have seen the local attractions, what else will there be to do?

That beach that was so beautiful during the week you spent there will lose its appeal when you see it every day, and it may not be so inviting during the winter.

One RetireFabulously.com reader bought a condo in a popular vacation destination. She discovered to her disappointment that many of the other units in her development were purchased as investment properties and were being rented out on Airbnb or VRBO. She had a difficult time developing a network of friends in her area because most of the other people came and went every week. A steady flow of vacationers can also lead to more late-night partying and less concern for the maintenance of the property.

So, what's really important?

Before you think too much about where you would like to retire, I encourage you to devote considerable thought to what you want to do during your retirement. How do you envision spending each day? What activities to you plan to engage in?

I covered this topic in great detail in my first book, *Design Your Dream Retirement: How to Envision, Plan For, and Enjoy the Best Retirement Possible*. I won't go into depth here, but I encourage you to download the free Retirement Visualization Guide from RetireFabulously.com/quest-resources. It will ask you dozens of questions that will help you envision how you want to live out your retirement and clarify what's really important for you.

Once you have a clear picture of what you want to do during your retirement, you'll be able to evaluate each place you consider in terms of whether it can provide the amenities, activities, and resources you will need.

In a 2018 poll, readers of RetireFabulously.com rated the importance of numerous criteria for choosing a good retirement location. These factors are presented in the order of importance, based upon the survey results.

There was considerable variation among the poll responses, which is to be expected. Your priorities won't match this list exactly, either. However, this list should help you gain more clarity on what is important to you. It will probably suggest some things you haven't thought about until now.

1. Climate and weather

Many people choose to move to warmer climates after they retire. While there are nice cities in colder climates that offer excellent amenities for retirees, the fact remains that wintry weather conditions present greater challenges as you age. Shoveling snow will become more physically demanding and the potential for injury is greater. Still, plenty of people retire to colder climates or choose to remain where they currently live, and they make it work.

In a few chapters, we'll discuss best places to retire lists and whether or not they are useful. (Spoiler alert: not so much.) Very few of them consider climate and weather among their criteria. For most people who took this survey, this is one of the main reasons people move in retirement.

Think about how much rain or snow you are willing to accept. What are the minimum and maximum temperatures you are willing to tolerate?

2. Safety

Most people want to live somewhere where the crime rate is low.

The good news is that crime rates in the United States reached a high plateau in the 1970s and '80s. From the early '90s to the present, crime rates across all categories have been on a steady downward trend. Both violent crimes and physical crimes have plummeted to half of what they were in the '70s and '80s – sometimes more. Crime rates today are comparable to what they were around 1960. This data comes from the Uniform Crime Report[2] produced by the FBI every year. Data supporting this conclusion has been presented by the Pew Research Center, the Brennan Center for Justice, Statistica, and Wikipedia. Check out the crime data for almost any city on city-data.com. You'll see that, in most places, it's going down.

The bad news, aside from the fact that crime exists at all and there has been a disturbing increase in random mass shootings, is that the United States still has higher crime rates than many countries in the world, particularly those in Europe, Oceania, Asia, and some countries in the Middle East.

Like many other issues in society today, crime seems worse than it really is because it gets attention on the news and on the Internet.

Some politicians make fighting crime one of their talking points on the campaign trail. That's low-hanging fruit for any politician. Like the

---

[2] https://ucr.fbi.gov/crime-in-the-u.s

news media and the Internet, these politicians imply that it's a worse problem than it actually is. It plays on people's fears in order to get votes. Once elected, the politician may do little or nothing throughout his or her term to fight crime, then claim success when the crime rates have decreased further during his or her term.

It's fine to compare the crime statistics for places you are considering, but keep in mind that crime rates vary widely in different areas of the same city. So, while a large city might appear to have a higher crime rate (relatively speaking), there are many areas in that city that are perfectly safe. In the United States, CommunityCrimeMap.com is a terrific resource for assessing crime at the neighborhood level.

In any case, you probably aren't going to begin the search for your ideal retirement destination by searching for the places with the lowest crime rate. You should begin by finding areas that offer the lifestyle, amenities, and surroundings you want to enjoy. Then you can check the crime rate and refine your search to the relatively safer neighborhoods.

3. Proximity to healthcare

In my opinion, this is one of the most important factors you should consider when deciding where to live.

This factor may not seem particularly important during your earlier retirement years when you are healthy, active, and have little need for medical services beyond routine doctor visits. But you should consider the quality of and proximity to good healthcare when selecting a place to live to prevent moving again when you need to avail yourself of medical care more often.

This is one of the main reasons I want to discourage you from living in a remote location. Should an emergency arise, you won't want to live an hour away from the nearest hospital. Keep in mind that if you need to call an ambulance, it will take an additional hour for the ambulance to get to you. Even in non-emergency situations, being a long way from doctor's offices can be a challenge if you need transportation.

US News[3] publishes an annual ranking of best hospitals throughout the United States. You may wish to assess the quality of the hospitals in each area you are considering. The link is on the Resources webpage.

---

[3] https://health.usnews.com/best-hospitals/area

4. Cost of living

The local cost of living plays a big role in the lifestyle you can afford in retirement. Remember to consider your anticipated living situation when examining this data, such as what activities you want to participate in, whether you will buy or rent, and whether you plan to own cars or rely upon public transportation. We'll cover cost of living in greater detail in an upcoming chapter.

5. Cultural amenities

If you enjoy art, theater, concerts, or other forms of culture, you will want to choose a place where those opportunities are readily available. Colleges and universities are good sources for the performing arts. The performances are usually free or inexpensive, and the students will appreciate having an audience. Larger universities attract some nationally-known performers, too.

If you prefer professional-level venues and performances, you should investigate whether places you are considering offer that. If you have favorite musical artists or groups, do they ever perform in the area you are considering when they go on tour?

If you hope to participate in culture-based activities, try to determine whether sufficient opportunities are available. For example, is the area you are looking at large enough to support a community band, chorus, or theatre? Do any art centers offer art classes and member shows?

6. Low taxes

When you consider the tax burden of a place you are considering moving to, be sure to look at the overall picture. While some states may have no income tax or no sales tax, other taxes will be higher. States need to collect their revenue one way or another. Your income sources and spending patterns will factor into how a state's tax structure will impact you.

Also keep in mind that sometimes places with higher taxes provide better services, and those may be services you'll want to avail yourself of. In most cases, you get what you pay for. There's a chapter in this book devoted to identifying high-tax and low-tax states.

But just as low cost of living shouldn't be your only consideration for where you live, neither should you move to an area only because the taxes are lower. There are a dozen or so states in which taxes are noticeably higher than most other states, but aside from those, you probably won't realize significant tax savings from one state to the next – especially since many states do not tax Social Security and the rest of your income will probably keep you in lower tax brackets.

So, select your short list of retirement destinations based on the factors that will keep you happy and satisfied on a day-to-day basis. Then you can eliminate the places that are in high-tax states.

7. Recreational amenities

The recreational activities you plan to enjoy during your retirement should significantly inform your choice of retirement destination. You should consider not only whether the facilities for your favorite activities exist, but also how much of the year you will be able to enjoy them. This ties in with weather and climate, above.

For example, if you're an avid golfer, there may be nice golf courses in Montana, but the golf season will be a lot shorter than it is in warmer states.

8. Proximity to a major airport

If traveling is part of the retirement lifestyle you are looking forward to, you will appreciate being close to an airport that offers flights to a wide selection of destinations. The same convenience will benefit your friends and relatives who will come to visit you.

9. Political/social climate

Regardless of where your views fall on the political spectrum, you should consider whether you will be comfortable if you move to an environment where the majority of people are of a different political persuasion. Everyone is entitled to their political and social views, but conversations in social settings may be less enjoyable if everyone else's views are significantly different than yours.

You can get a feel for the political climate on city-data.com, which shows how each city voted in the last few presidential elections. You should also consider existing laws on issues of concern to you, and whether the state and local governments are likely to enact legislation that you would agree with.

Similarly, when you visit and interact with the local people, try to sense whether they are open-minded, welcoming, and friendly. If you sense that most people fit into different demographics and the social network seems tight and insular, it may be more difficult for you to fit in as an outsider.

10. Avoidance of discrimination

If you identify with a minority group of any kind, you are already well aware that there are places in the United States and other parts of the world where you will be more likely to encounter discrimination.

11. Presence of diverse people

Workplaces across the United States and some other countries have become more diverse over the past few decades. If you have worked in such an environment, you have probably grown to appreciate interacting with a wide variety of people, as well as enjoying a broad range of restaurants and cultural offerings.

You may prefer to surround yourself with people of varying ages and demographics, rather than settling into a community where everyone else looks like you.

12. Availability and quality of senior services

Just like with medical care, you may not need these services for the first decade or more of your retirement. But someday, you probably will. Try to discover whether an area you are considering has a senior center or organizations that provide services to seniors, such as Meals on Wheels, social groups, activities, classes, and help with transportation.

There's another dimension to the issue of senior services.

The oldest-aged US state is Maine, with a median age of 44.6 years. New Hampshire and Vermont aren't far behind, at 43.2 and 42.6, respectively. In comparison, the nationwide median age in the US is 38.1.

Maine is now facing an acute shortage of home care aides.[4] In some areas, people who require home care aren't receiving it because agencies cannot recruit enough staff to serve the need. Many younger people have left the state to seek better employment prospects and lower cost of living. Home care aide has traditionally been a low-paying job, and the younger workers who remain in the state can make better money working in other fields, even fast food.

The ratio of doctors and nurses to the overall population is decreasing too. Doctors and nurses are retiring faster than new practitioners are coming to the state, while the state's population continues to skew older.

Maine is on the forefront of this trend, but other states with higher median ages are expected to experience the same shortages. This would include New Hampshire, Vermont, West Virginia, Florida, Connecticut, Pennsylvania, Delaware, and Montana – all of which have median ages of 40 or older.

The same conditions exist in rural areas of other states. As healthcare costs escalate, many small rural hospitals have closed, forcing residents to travel farther to receive medical care. Time and distance could be critical in the case of a serious illness or injury.

In general, places where the population is declining and younger people are migrating away to seek better employment prospects are more likely to experience shortages of people to provide elder care.

13. Proximity to loved ones

If you have children or grandchildren, you will probably want to be able to see them often. The same applies for your closest friends. Hopefully, in later years your family and friends will be part of your support network.

Proximity to children and grandchildren is one of the most important factors for some people.

---

[4] https://www.washingtonpost.com/business/economy/this-will-be-catastrophic-maine-families-face-elder-boom-worker-shortage-in-preview-of-nations-future/2019/08/14/7cecafc6-bec1-11e9-b873-63ace636af08_story.html

However, keep in mind that your family members may move to follow job opportunities or for other reasons. Will you be willing and able to move to follow them? Can you afford to?

As much as you love your children and grandchildren, you may not be happy in the long run if you live in a place that you dislike just because they live there.

14. Public transportation

There may come a time when you can't drive any more. Even if you can, you may prefer to take public transportation if the city you are considering has a good system. Websites such as walkscore.com can provide useful information in this regard.

However, keep in mind that public transportation, especially during rush hour, can be crowded and challenging for older people.

Some communities provide transport vans for people with accessibility needs. Try to find out if a place you are considering offers this service.

Services such as Uber and Lyft may be a better option than public transportation in some cases.

15. Availability and quality of local assisted living and nursing homes

During the early years of your retirement, looking at assisted living and nursing home facilities is probably the last thing you want to do. But as you evaluate potential places to live, it helps to determine if the facilities in your area are places you would be willing to live someday. You don't have to pick one, and places may come and go or change over the years, but it still helps to know if there are good facilities in your area.

Years from now, you may not be able to make a long-distance move to an assisted living or nursing home in another part of the state or country unless you have assistance from younger family members or friends. When the time comes, you probably won't be in a position to conduct a lengthy search for the best facility across multiple geographic areas – you will have to limit your search to places in your area.

Plus, by staying in the same area, you will still have access to your support network and you can continue to use the same doctors and dentists you have established a relationship with.

There are two resources linked on the Resources webpage that will assist you in assessing the cost and quality of senior services across the country – the Genworth Cost of Care Survey[5] and the Long-Term Services & Supports State Scorecard.[6]

16. Local college or university

Having a college or university nearby offers several advantages. They usually offer concerts and theatre productions for free or at low cost. Many higher education institutions offer seniors the opportunity to attend classes on a non-graded basis for free or at low cost.

Community colleges, in particular, are inexpensive and make it easy to attend classes regardless of whether or not you are seeking a degree. Many offer bands or choruses that anyone in the community can join for the cost of one credit-hour of tuition, as well as classes in subjects such as languages and computer skills.

Many people underestimate this benefit. I strongly encourage living in an area that has a university or a good community college. In addition to the advantages they offer for continuing education and free cultural enrichment, their presence in an area gives the area some economic stability during downturns.

17. Concentration of other seniors

Do you want to live in a community that is made up entirely of other retirees, or would you prefer to live among a wider cross-section of people?

55+ active adult communities have been a popular option for the past sixty years, but some data suggest that the popularity of these places will diminish in the future. The fact that this criterion placed so low among RetireFabulously.com readers suggests that this trend is already underway.

---

[5] https://www.genworth.com/aging-and-you/finances/cost-of-care.html
[6] http://www.longtermscorecard.org/

I'm not a fan of these communities, but that's just me. They are an excellent choice for some people. But try not to simply assume that you should move to a retirement community just because that's what so many other retired people do. There are many other options.

A section of this book is devoted to living in age-restricted 55+ active adult communities, including a discussion of the pros and cons.

18. Same-sex marriage recognized
19. Availability and quality of LGBT-friendly health services
20. LGBT Community

Not surprisingly, the last three categories ranked much higher among Lesbian, Gay, Bisexual, and Transgender (LGBT) respondents, and were the lowest concerns for almost everyone else.

———

The survey included an opportunity for respondents to suggest other important criteria, and some people offered good suggestions, including:

- Plentiful options for outdoor activities
- High walkability
- Good local restaurants and produce markets
- Friendliness of local people
- Local religious community of your faith
- Adequate shopping nearby
- Proximity to water
- Proximity to mountains
- Ease of driving
- Aesthetically pleasing / natural beauty
- Peaceful and quiet
- Space for a garden and/or animals
- Air and water quality
- Pet-friendly
- Abundance of good handymen and service providers
- Availability of military facilities (for veterans)
- A culture that respects all women
- Potential impact of climate change

- Appreciating property values
- English widely spoken and understood

The bottom line is that your Retirement Utopia is the place where you will best be able to enjoy doing all the things you want to do day-to-day, in pleasant surroundings, in a place you can afford.

Chapter 4

Taking a Long-Term View

When you start thinking about where you would like to live after you retire, you are probably focused primarily on how you envision living your life for the foreseeable future, perhaps the first five or ten years of your retirement.

But what about when you get older?

As you age, your needs and your abilities will change. Generally, you'll move through three phases of your retirement: your go-go years, your slow-go years, and your no-go years.

You may, indeed, spend the first five or ten years of your retirement playing golf, hiking, traveling, and pretty much doing everything you enjoy.

But sooner or later, despite your best efforts to stay healthy and fit, you'll enter a period in which you can no longer participate in as many physical activities. You'll start needing more medical care and support. Transportation and mobility needs may arise.

Then, as you enter your final phase, you may need to consider hiring home care aides or moving into an assisted living community and perhaps a skilled nursing home. You may need to avail yourself of the senior services that are hopefully available in your area.

How will the area in which you live stack up then?

That cabin in the mountains may be a two-hour drive away from the doctors you need to see.

That house on the shore of a quiet peaceful lake may become too far removed from the stores where you need to shop after you can no longer drive.

That second-story condo near the beach may become difficult to navigate once you have trouble climbing stairs.

It's important to evaluate any place you are considering moving to with the perspective of how that area will serve your needs throughout the remainder of your life.

It's impossible to know how an area will change in ten, twenty, or even thirty years. Still, you can look at trends and extend them into the future.

For example, if an area is growing and experiencing a boom in new construction, that area will probably still have vitality in the foreseeable future. If an area is already decaying and the population is decreasing, you can assume that the area will probably grow worse in the coming years.

The exception is urban areas of prosperous larger cities. In many cities, the areas in and near the downtown are being rebuilt with condos, apartments, restaurants, and retail establishments. This gentrification is being driven by today's Millennials, who are opting for in-town living as opposed to suburban living. These younger people are less likely to own cars (either by choice or because they can't afford them) and prefer to live in an area that is highly walkable and accessible to public transit.

While it may be a stretch to envision Millennials and retirees living side-by-side, many of these same values and criteria are a good fit for retired people.

The economic stability and level of prosperity of an area are important considerations. Even if you're no longer working, the area's unemployment rate is important to consider. In an area with high unemployment, crime will rise, property values may fall, and area businesses will suffer and ultimately close. The community's tax revenue will also suffer, which means they will have to raise taxes, cut back on services, or both.

Areas with future-facing industries such as high-tech and medical research should continue to grow and prosper, while areas that rely on manufacturing will continue to decline. Cities with large universities, government employment, and financial services are likely to remain steadier throughout varying economic cycles.

One of the most important considerations for choosing where to retire is the average age of the area's population. This factor is rarely mentioned, but it is becoming increasingly important as the Baby Boomer generation continues to grow older, retire, and live longer. The shortage of home care aides, doctors, and nurses in Maine (discussed in the previous chapter) is an excellent example of this.

Chapter 5

Best Places to Retire Lists – Fact, Fiction, or Fantasy?

There are now hundreds of Best Places to Retire lists on the Internet, as well as some Worst Places to Retire lists. They all offer different results. With so many contradictory lists, how are you to make sense of it all?

Best Places to Live lists have a long history. Money magazine has published a Best Places to Live list annually for decades. Oddly, the lists come out differently every year. Regional booms and recessions will certainly impact any city over time, but could things really change that much in one year?

The explanation, of course, lies with which selection criteria the list creators consider and how much weight they place on the various factors. You don't have to tweak the criteria or the weighting very much for the list to change significantly.

Some lists are created by analyzing data, and the data categories which are selected vary widely. For example, one list may be driven by low cost without regard to weather or climate. Another might sort by how many people in a location are over 65 or by longevity. Others are created based on paying the lowest taxes or most sunny days.

Then there are lists that are based on such subjective criteria such as 'livability' and 'quality of life.' How do you define and measure that?

Other lists use various 'well-being' factors, such as the percentage of people who smoke, consume soda, or are overweight. To me, these are of little value. The lifestyle habits of the majority of the population have no direct impact on you. Whether you live a healthy or unhealthy lifestyle is completely up to you, and you can make those choices no matter where you live.

It's useful to consider the source. Some of the more popular lists are published by entities that have no direct experience with retirement. For example, Bankrate and Wallethub are financial services companies that offer credit cards and loans. Smart Assets promotes financial advisors. These firms and many others use these lists as magnets for promoting their products. This strategy works – these lists are often cited in many other articles.

Yet, because they are created using limited criteria and arbitrary weightings, they produce wildly different and often questionable results.

I suspect some lists are just created on the fly by content marketing writers facing a publishing deadline. And whenever they are presented in slideshow format, as many of them are, you know that they are also serving the purpose of generating ad revenue.

InternationalLiving.com releases an annual World's Best Places to Retire list. Their methodology takes into account many criteria, such as cost of buying and renting, overall cost of living, quality of healthcare, and climate. Still, much of their input comes from their correspondents located in these countries and is subjective. And while International Living does provide a lot of valuable information and interesting reading, my perception is that they view the expat world through rose-colored glasses. Their articles wax eloquent about how beautiful and inexpensive a featured country is, yet they rarely mention any drawbacks to living there.

Also keep in mind that websites such as International Living are in business to sell books. This isn't a bad thing, but it does cloud the objectivity of the information they offer. They succeed by selling a dream.

Would you decide to move to a city, a state, or a foreign country just because it ranked highly on one or more lists? Of course not.

So, do these lists have any value or are they completely useless?

I think they offer some value, for several reasons:

- They may suggest places you haven't thought of, which may be very good options for you.
- They stimulate curiosity and fantasy. Is the grass really greener in an intriguing new place? Is there really a Retirement Utopia out there somewhere?
- They offer a sanity check for places you may be considering. You may gain information about a potential retirement destination that you might not otherwise discover until you have lived there for several months. Information about factors such as tax rates, quality of medical care, senior services available, and many other criteria may serve to disqualify a place you're considering or verify that you're making a good choice.
- They're fun, even if it's just for their 'WTF' factor. At least half of the cities named leave me scratching my head and thinking, "I wouldn't want to live there!"

If you know you want to move but you really have no idea where you want to end up, lists can provide some ideas. Even if you have one or two destinations in mind, lists can open up other possibilities that may suit you better.

During the time I spent researching and writing this book, as well as the entire time I have been writing articles for RetireFabulously.com, I have seen a lot of lists. While I am pretty well-traveled and I've been to 47 of the 50 states and 28 countries, these lists have introduced me to a lot of places I knew little about. Some of them are interesting and worth considering.

It's fine to look at lists, but don't buy into any of them as the most authoritative, definitive resource. Do plenty of research and follow up with several visits of at least a week. For international destinations, longer visits are a good idea.

Chapter 6

The Great Data Crunch

There's so much data available and so many factors to consider that trying to search for your Retirement Utopia by gathering and analyzing data will get overwhelming very quickly. You'll suffer from 'paralysis by analysis.'

The best example of trying to determine the best places to retire by analyzing data is the Milken Institute's *Best Cities for Successful Aging*[7] report released in 2014 and updated in 2017. This is arguably the most well-researched, fact-based, statistically-driven study ever conducted on the topic of best retirement cities and towns. The Institute's staff gathered and analyzed a large amount of data across many categories. This isn't the result of opinion polls. Their methodology and their results are thoroughly presented.

Yet, their rankings of the 100 best large cities and 281 best small cities are curious at best. Most cities at the top of both lists are in the center of the country, while most sunny, warm places that are traditional retiree favorites came out at the bottom of their rankings. Why do their results differ so much from where retirees are actually moving?

The results all depend on what factors are considered and how they are weighted, and that's how this report ends up with such curious rankings. Some factors they considered have very little to do with

---

[7] http://successfulaging.milkeninstitute.org/

quality of retirement life, such as the number of banks, the percentage of adults who drink soda, and the level of college enrollment. All of these inconsequential factors crowd out some of the more important ones. In this study, weather counts for just 4.5 percent of the total weight and house prices and rentals count for just 2.7 percent, but these two factors are high on most people's list of criteria.

Clearly, finding the best retirement destination is not a purely data-driven exercise.

There is no one-size-fits-all ideal retirement destination, and attempting to identify one strictly by data would yield the same answer for everyone.

In many ways, choosing the best place for you to retire is like choosing your sweetheart. In both cases, you can make lists of the qualities that your potential mate or your potential place to live must have and other qualities that are nice to have. Then you meet that special someone or visit that special place, and you fall in love. It's a highly subjective and emotional choice that sometimes flies in the face of logical reasoning and statistical analysis.

All humans make decisions based on emotion. We use facts and logic too, but these take a back seat to emotion. Facts and logic can fine-tune our decisions or, more often, verify information and convince ourselves that we are making the right choice. A thorough look at facts may reveal unfavorable information that becomes a deal-breaker.

Making decisions based on your emotions is not a bad thing. In many cases, you should trust your gut instincts. You'll know when a place feels right and makes your heart sing.

But you should back up your emotional decision by doing as much research with your eyes wide open as you can. Don't allow yourself to be swept away by fanciful dreaming, alluring articles with enhanced photos, or slick marketing materials. Every place has some downsides. Find out what they are and decide whether or not you can live with them before you start packing and put your house on the market.

But where you retire will always be, first and foremost, an emotion-based decision. Very few people will decide to move someplace to retire simply because that place landed at the top of some Best Places to Retire list.

Neither are you going to commit to a retirement destination because it statistically works out to be the best place. So, save yourself hours of painstaking data gathering and plugging hundreds of data points into an Excel spreadsheet. Using data in a spreadsheet is a good idea for making a side-by-side comparison of a few finalists. It's good for creating a budget for living in a particular area.

But the bottom line is, retire to a place you love.

Here's the process I recommend for finding that special place – your Retirement Utopia.

1. Identify the criteria that are most important to you

As you read in the previous chapter, there are dozens of factors you can consider. The number of criteria that your ideal retirement destination must meet can easily become overwhelming. There is probably no place that meets all of your criteria. That's why it's so important to prioritize.

You may be able to identify your essential, most important criteria now, as well as some nice-to-have criteria.

But if you are not clear on your most important criteria, I have an exercise for you. On RetireFabulously.com/quest-resources, there is a downloadable file called *100 Questions to Answer Before You Move*. You may wish to print a copy for yourself and one for your spouse, if you have one. You might be surprised by how much your partner's priorities differ from yours.

After you have considered all these questions, you should be better able to identify the most important qualities and/or things your new area must have. Try to limit yourself to five must-have, deal-breaker criteria.

Then identify the qualities and/or things that would be nice for your new area to have. Hopefully, your retirement destination will have most of these criteria, but there might be one or two you would be willing to compromise on.

Some of the most important factors might be everyday things such as the ease of finding groceries you want or whether there's a good bookstore or jazz club in the area. These seemingly mundane considerations could have the biggest impact on how much you enjoy daily life in your new surroundings.

For example, a lovely condo overlooking the beach and the ocean on Kauai may seem like retiring in paradise. And no question, Kauai is beautiful (and expensive). But after you consider the factors that are most important to you, you will discover that there's no Costco on Kauai, there are few options for playing music, and flights in and out of Kauai are limited. Most travel you embark upon will require flying to Honolulu to connect to another flight of six hours or more that will take you where you want to go.

The point of this exercise is to try to establish your list of what's most important to you without being influenced by the characteristics of any places you already have in mind.

2. Create a short list

Chances are, you probably already have at least one place in mind. Maybe it's a place you visited on vacation (but again, I caution against this). Maybe it's a place you've heard others rave about or someplace you've seen in a magazine article. Or it could be someplace where friends or relatives have already moved, and they say they love it.

Unfortunately, there is no great computer application into which you can enter all your data and have it return the most ideal place(s) for you to retire. TopRetirements.com has an application called the Retirement Ranger which may be helpful.

If you are having trouble coming up with options, those Best Places to Retire lists may give you some ideas. I will suggest some options in the next section of this book.

Try to come up with five to ten. If you come up with more, that's okay. We'll eliminate some of them in the next step.

If you can only come up with one or two, ask yourself whether it would be helpful to expand your horizons and consider some more possibilities. But if you truly have your heart set on one place, at least be willing to put it through a rigorous, open-minded analysis of whether it really is a great place to retire for you.

For example, San Diego is a truly beautiful city with a pleasant climate and lots of things to see and do. It would be easy to convince yourself that San Diego is the only real choice for you. But you should honestly consider the realities that the cost of real estate there is very high, gasoline is expensive, and California is a high-tax state. Can you really afford to live there and still be able to travel and do the other things you hope to do after you retire?

3. Research each place to determine its suitability

Using the resources provided on RetireFabulously.com/quest-resources, try to determine, as objectively as possible, how well each place on your list meets the criteria you have established.

This step is difficult for two reasons.

First, it's easy to be influenced by confirmation bias. Confirmation bias happens when you allow yourself (sometimes subconsciously) to prioritize information that supports the conclusion you're hoping for and dismiss information that works against your desired conclusion.

For example, if you have your heart set on retiring to Key West, Florida, you may be happy to collect information about how many days of sunshine Key West enjoys each year and how many highly-rated restaurants are available on the island, while downplaying data about how expensive real estate is or how susceptible the area is to hurricanes.

The second reason this exercise is difficult is that research on some of your criteria won't yield clear yes-or-no answers. There's a lot of gray area. If one of your criteria is having a Costco within 25 miles, will you cross off a town that has a Costco 30 miles away?

At this point, hopefully you have worked your list down to a manageable size with perhaps five or fewer finalists. If you still have a lot of viable options on your list, try applying more criteria.

Similarly, if there are places on your list that are larger, non-specific areas (for example, Hawaii, the Gulf Coast, the Southwest), try to narrow your search to one or a few specific cities or towns in these areas.

4. Visit each place

There is no substitute for experiencing a place in person. Photos and stories on websites operated by retirement communities, a city or state's Chamber of Commerce, or Convention and Visitor's Bureau are going to present the place in the best possible light. Many photos are taken with filters or are tweaked using software. Places rarely look the same as they are represented in photos.

Many areas have Facebook groups where the local residents share information and ask for recommendations. Joining these groups can be informative, but this shouldn't be your only means of evaluating a city.

Sometimes these groups attract a lot of complainers. If you have questions, especially after visiting, you will probably get a lot of responses.

Try to spend at least a week there, not just a weekend.

If you have visited a place in the past on vacation or on a business trip, go again. Your focus should be different when you are evaluating the area as a place to live.

When you go, don't go as a tourist. Don't go to the beach and the tourist attractions. Rather than staying in a hotel, see if you can rent a house or apartment on Airbnb or VRBO.

Your objective is to experience the area as a resident to the greatest extent possible. How much you enjoy your retirement will be determined more by how your life plays out each day and less by the local attractions that you aren't likely to visit regularly.

In the next chapter, you will find a somewhat lengthy list of things to look for while you visit a city or town that is a potential retirement destination.

You will be able to gather a lot of data and factual information on your trip, but more importantly, you will get a gut feeling for whether you would be happy living in this place. You'll be able to sense, emotionally, whether or not you could see yourself living there.

5. Evaluate your finalists side-by-side

You will be able to downgrade or eliminate some of your choices based on the factual data you have collected and your first-hand impressions of the area.

But when it comes to selecting the winner, you will probably know in your heart which one is your favorite. Hopefully, it's the same place your spouse or partner wants. If not, hopefully there's at least one place near the top of your lists that you both like.

The primary benefit of this exercise is to help you identify what's most important, or to disqualify places that lack some qualities that are essential to you. It's easy to romanticize or get swept away by a beautiful place, but the more mundane factors that impact your everyday life will remain relevant long after the shininess of a place wears off.

Chapter 7

What to Look for When You Visit a Potential Retirement Destination

When you visit a place that you are seriously considering moving to, here are some things to consider. Some of these factors are objective, but many are subjective. Not all of them may be important to you.

The purpose of these suggestions is to prompt you to discover what it will be like to live in an area on a day-to-day basis, to the greatest extent possible. Remember, you're not going as a tourist.

- Go to the grocery stores and shopping malls and notice the selection and prices.
- Notice whether most shopping centers are fully occupied, or if there are a lot of empty storefronts and abandoned buildings.
- When you go to stores and shopping centers, are there security guards? If so, they are there for a reason.
- If you're a churchgoer, visit a church of your faith.
- If you are an avid reader, visit the local bookstores and libraries. The library is a very useful stop, because in addition to books it is likely to have a lot of other information about the community. See if it offers programs or classes that might be of interest.
- Visit the local senior center and learn what services they offer.

- Ride the public transit.
- Evaluate the ease of walking or riding a bicycle.
- Eat at the local restaurants, not the national chains or tourist-oriented places, unless you are most likely to eat at the chains once you move there. Do you have to ask for a key to use the restroom?
- Drive throughout the area and get a feel for the neighborhoods. Once you have identified neighborhoods where you could envision yourself living, how close are stores, restaurants, and medical facilities?
- Tour a few homes for sale or apartments for rent in neighborhoods where you think you might live if you were to move there.
- Gather some local publications that are distributed for free at the entrances to grocery stores, restaurants, or other well-traveled places. Learn what issues concern local residents and what local activities are mentioned. What kind of events or festivals does the area have? Publications that contain local real estate listings are useful as well.
- Talk to some local residents if you can. Ask what they like most and least about living there. Try to gauge the extent to which they are welcoming of outsiders.
- Find a few assisted living facilities or nursing homes and see whether they are places you would want to live someday in the future if necessary. Walk into the local hospital and look around.
- Depending on your interests, try to determine what local clubs and organizations exist. For example, if you're into community theatre, what are the options?
- Depending on your interests, are there outdoor recreational options that will satisfy you?
- Are the public amenities, such as roads and parks, well maintained? Does the area have a litter problem?
- Notice the age and condition of houses and buildings. Especially in older cities, is the area staying rejuvenated, or does everything seem old and tired?
- Is there a lot of graffiti?
- Do you see a lot of homeless people and beggars?

- What things are there to see or do on an ongoing basis? What is there to explore within 100 miles? Keep in mind that many attractions are places you will visit just once, or perhaps only occasionally when you are entertaining out-of-town guests. Places like museums, galleries, or other attractions where the displays change over time will provide more interest in the long run.

This checklist of factors to consider when you visit a potential retirement destination may be downloaded from the Resources webpage.

PART THREE

Best and Worst Places to Retire in the United States

Chapter 8

Where Can You Pay the Least Taxes?

Everyone wants to pay as little tax as possible, but just as I don't recommend that you choose a place to live based primarily on lowest cost of living, neither do I recommend that you choose a state only because it has the lowest tax rates.

It's much more important to think about the overall quality of life than how much you are paying in taxes.

After reading the last few chapters, hopefully you have created a short list of places you'd like to retire based on all the other qualitative factors that are important to you. Now you can consider eliminating places in states with high tax burdens or use the tax burden as a tie-breaker.

Trying to compare states side-by-side on taxes is complicated, since each state has its own mix of rates for income, sales, property, and other taxes such as excise and inheritance taxes. States tax or do not tax Social Security, public pension income, and private pension income.

Many articles and lists place a lot of preference on states that have no sales tax or no income tax. As it turns out, this isn't such a big deal. States need to collect revenue one way or another. The Tax Foundation's

Sources of State and Local Tax Collection[8] chart shows the mix of sales tax, income tax, and property tax you'll pay in each state.

The United States averages for what percentage of each state's tax revenue comes from each source are:

Property tax – 31.5%

Sales tax – 23.6%

Individual income – 23.5%

This means that 78.6 percent of all state tax revenue comes from these three sources. The rest are corporate and other taxes, such as excise taxes (alcohol, tobacco, motor vehicles, utilities, and licenses), severance taxes, stock transfer taxes, estate and gift taxes, and other miscellaneous taxes. Most of those other taxes are paid by individuals too.

Oregon has no sales tax, but they collect 32.0 percent of their taxes in the form of property tax (about the national average) and 41.7 percent in the form of income tax (significantly above the national average). That totals 73.7 percent, which isn't too much under the national average. Their other taxes are higher too, so the lack of sales taxes is negated by higher taxes in other forms.

Texas has no individual income tax, but they collect 43.8 percent of their taxes in the form of property tax and 35.4 percent in the form of sales tax, for a total of 79.2 percent. Texas also levies no income tax on corporations, so all of their remaining revenue comes from other taxes – most of which are paid by individuals.

So, a state that collects no sales tax or no income tax isn't necessarily a lower-tax state. They have to get their money from somewhere.

There's one case where residing in a state with no income tax is advantageous, and that's if you live full-time in an RV and travel around the country in it. In this case, you can establish residence in a no-income-tax state. You won't be paying property tax there if you don't own property, and you will pay sales tax in whatever state you happen to be in at the time.

When you consider property tax, remember that rates are only part of the equation. You should also consider the cost of the home you expect to purchase, which varies widely across the country and often within

---

[8] https://files.taxfoundation.org/20190715165329/Facts-Figures-2019-How-Does-Your-State-Compare.pdf

each state. The actual property tax you'll pay is the home's assessed value times the property tax rate. So, a higher tax rate on a less expensive home might result in a lower tax payment than a lower tax rate on a more expensive home.

If you're planning to rent, you're still paying property tax, you're just paying it indirectly. The landlord is passing his or her tax bill on to you as part of your rent. If property taxes go up, you can bet your rent will go up.

TaxFoundation.org is one of the best places to find information about taxes throughout the United States. The Tax Foundation publishes a booklet each year called *How Does Your State Compare*. This downloadable PDF contains a lot of useful tax information.

For example, there's a chart that lists each state's Tax Freedom Day. Tax Freedom Day represents how long into the year Americans work before they have earned enough money to pay all federal, state, and local taxes for the year. The earlier the Tax Freedom Day comes, the less tax you would pay if you lived in that state.

This booklet also lists each state's income tax rates by income level. Some states have progressively higher tax rates at various income brackets and some tax all people at the same rate.

There are also charts which show state tax rates on items like gasoline, beer, wine, liquor, groceries, candy, soda, and even marijuana where it's legal. This may be of interest depending on how much you expect to drive (if at all) and your other consumption habits.

State Debt per Capita is a useful chart. A state with a high debt burden is more likely to increase taxes in the future. This figure also means that states have to use more of their tax revenue to pay interest, which leaves less for delivering services. Not surprisingly, the states with the highest debt are usually among the states with the highest taxes. These are: Massachusetts, Connecticut, Rhode Island, New Jersey, New York, Hawaii, New Hampshire, Vermont, Illinois, Delaware, and Maryland.

Another factor that is worth considering is whether a state taxes Social Security income and pension income (public and/or private). These taxes disproportionately impact retired people.

By now, your head is probably spinning. How are you supposed to realistically compare states and determine which are the worst for taxes?

The more websites you visit and articles you read, the more conflicting information you find.

Here are two of the better lists.

The Tax Foundation's Tax Freedom Day ranking, mentioned above, lists these 17 states with Tax Freedom Days equal to or later than the national average, which is April 19. This means that these are the states with the highest tax burdens. Note that these rankings apply to all taxpayers, not just retirees.

May 14: New York
May 3: Connecticut, New Jersey, District of Columbia
April 29: Illinois
April 27: Minnesota
April 26: Massachusetts
April 24: North Dakota, Rhode Island
April 23: California, Vermont
April 21: Wyoming
April 20: Hawaii, Maine
April 19: Maryland, Pennsylvania, Washington, Wisconsin

Kiplinger[9] has a state-by-state guide to taxes on retirees, and they divide states into five quintiles based on their tax friendliness.

Their 10 least tax-friendly states for retirees: Minnesota, Connecticut, Kansas, Vermont, Nebraska, New Mexico, Utah, Maryland, Indiana, and Wisconsin.

The second tier of tax-unfriendly states (in alphabetical order): Arkansas, Iowa, Massachusetts, Michigan, Montana, New York, North Carolina, Oklahoma, Oregon, Rhode Island, and West Virginia.

Note that Kiplinger's list of tax unfriendly states differs somewhat from the Tax Federation's Tax Freedom Day list. That is probably because this list takes into account how taxes impact retirees with regard to whether states tax Social Security, public pensions, and private pensions, as well as tax breaks states might offer to retirees.

Smart Asset[10] also has a rating of states based on their tax-friendliness as well as a brief summary of each state's tax structure with

---

[9] https://www.kiplinger.com/tool/retirement/T055-S001-state-by-state-guide-to-taxes-on-retirees/index.php
[10] https://smartasset.com/retirement/retirement-taxes

regard to retirement income and a calculator which allows you to determine how much tax you'll pay in each city and state.

Not surprisingly, Smart Asset's assessment of how tax-friendly or tax-unfriendly states are is different from both of the lists above.

Visit RetireFabulously.com/quest-resources for links to all of the articles and websites mentioned above.

Despite everything I've covered here about taxes, remember that tax rates aren't a major factor in determining whether you will be happy living in a given place. Besides, even if you pay higher taxes in a place that otherwise has a very reasonable cost of living, you might still find that you can afford to live in that place.

Chapter 9

A Quick Look at Each State

In this section I will present a high-level overview of each state and offer a few suggestions for places that might make a good retirement destination. If you haven't yet settled on a few finalists for your Retirement Utopia, this section might suggest some possibilities.

I have been studying the topic of places to retire for several years and have read more articles, read more comments in discussion forums, and scratched my head at more lists that I could possibly count. I certainly can't claim to be the ultimate expert, but I have processed a lot of information.

I have tried to keep these recommendations as neutral and objective as possible, but inevitably some personal biases have slipped in.

I admit I tend to favor medium to large cities (or places that are within a half-hour of them), places which offer a wide variety of options for things to do, places where all types of people would be welcome, university cities, and places that seem well-positioned to thrive in the coming years.

For some of the largest cities, the best choices for retirement are often in the suburbs.

I have avoided suggesting places that are expensive, remote, potentially unsafe, and in general decline.

Most states are not homogenous. There are cities of varying sizes, rural areas, and often there are different climates and weather patterns. Socio-political characteristics can vary widely across a state. The cost of living in different areas of a state sometimes vary widely.

Tax rates are about the only thing that is constant across a state, and even sales tax rates can vary in different cities or counties. So, it's problematic to make generalizations about an entire state.

While I don't place too much stock in Best (or Worst) Places to Retire lists, if a place shows up on lists frequently it probably has something going for it.

Here are several important caveats to keep in mind.

One of my main sources of information about these places is city-data.com. Even though their data is good, it's not perfect. Errors do creep in. At one point, city-data.com claimed that in Madison, Wisconsin – which is otherwise a low-crime city – one out of every 30 citizens was a registered sex offender. This was obviously an error and it has since been corrected.

For cities with large universities, the presence of a lot of students will skew the statistics on average income and percentage of people who live in poverty.

Remember: crime statistics do not apply uniformly across a city. A larger city might show a crime rate that is higher than average, but many parts of town are perfectly safe. Communitycrimemap.com is an excellent resource for assessing crime in an area you are considering.

TopRetirements.com is an excellent resource for finding out how people who live in a place actually like it. That website has many articles with dozens or even hundreds of comments from readers sharing their personal experiences. Of course, those comments reflect widely divergent perspectives, and many commenters won't have the same criteria and priorities you do, but reading the discussions is often informative.

With all that said, let's take a quick tour around the wonderfully diverse United States of America. There is truly something for everybody, and there are certainly some great places for you.

New England

New England is lovely. The coastlines and mountains are serene and beautiful. Many of the cities and towns are charming and quaint. The town squares, covered bridges, and beautiful old houses combine to offer a Norman Rockwell-ish ambiance that seems so comfortable, inviting, and livable.

Unfortunately, on a practical level, New England presents a lot of disadvantages as a place to retire. Except for New Hampshire, state taxes are among the highest in the nation. In most areas, real estate is expensive. The winters are cold and snowy.

The New England states are also among the oldest – with Maine, New Hampshire, Vermont, and Connecticut having some of the highest median ages in the country. As discussed earlier, this has contributed to a shortage of healthcare and senior services professionals in some areas.

High tax rates are a disincentive for corporations to move to or stay in the area, and the high cost of living is prompting a migration of younger workers to other areas of the country.

All of this portends an uncertain economic future for most of New England, aside from Boston and its surrounding area.

Connecticut

Of all the New England states, Connecticut is the most problematic. The state is deeply in debt. It has the second-highest property tax rate in the nation paired with generally expensive real estate, so you'll pay a lot of tax on your house. Its corporate tax rates are among the highest, so employers such as General Electric and Aetna have moved out, and more are likely to follow.

Over time, the state government has made some labor-related, tax-related, and spending-related policy mistakes that have contributed significantly to the state's malaise.

With regard to retirement income, Connecticut taxes public and private pensions, but not military pensions. It taxes Social Security for couples earning over $60,000.

Maine

Maine has high taxes and relatively high cost of living, although it's less expensive than most of the rest of New England. Maine's shortage of healthcare professionals is worse in rural areas and less pronounced in cities.

Portland, the state's largest city, may be your best choice as a place to live. It is home to 20 percent of Maine's 1.3 million residents and, as such, has more to offer. Real estate prices are higher here, though.

Aside from that, there are many charming seaside towns such as Ogunquit, but they are generally more expensive and they experience seasonal variations in population.

Massachusetts

Massachusetts has high property and income tax. There is only one income tax bracket, which means everybody pays 5.1%. Cost of living is among the highest in the nation, too, but the state becomes more affordable as you move west.

The cities and towns situated along Interstate 91 are sometimes referred to as the "knowledge corridor" due to the number of universities and colleges in the area, which are conducive to lifelong learning and cultural offerings.

Northampton, in particular, has long been known as a haven for creative types and for its reputation for being welcoming of LGBT people.

Springfield is rated highly by Milken for good healthcare for older citizens as well as high funding for independent aging and transportation. Springfield and nearby Chicopee offer lower real estate prices than most of the rest of the state.

New Hampshire

New Hampshire is the exception to the high-tax reputation of New England and, depending on the area, it's relatively affordable. New Hampshire has no sales or income tax, although dividends and interest are taxed. New Hampshire collects most of its tax through real estate, which is among the highest in the nation. It's also more politically balanced than the rest of New England which leans Democratic.

Much of New Hampshire's population is clustered in the southeastern part of the state, near its short coastline and Boston. Nashua, while still a bit pricey, offers a more economical and tax-friendly option for living in the greater Boston area. Manchester, Concord, Dover, and other cities in this region aren't overly expensive and enjoy low crime rates.

Rhode Island

Rhode Island has one of the highest tax burdens in the country. Real estate taxes are high, and all Social Security and pension income is taxed.

If you're looking to call Rhode Island home, check out Pawtucket, Cranston, and Warwick. Each of these cities of about 80,000 is near Providence and offers reasonable housing prices and low crime.

Vermont

Vermont is beautiful, but it has high property and income taxes and high cost of living. Social Security and pension income are taxed. Most towns are small (only Burlington has over 20,000 people), and no one in particular stands out as a noteworthy choice.

Mid-Atlantic

Delaware

Many residents of the mid-Atlantic and New England states flock to Delaware for its laid-back feel, pleasant weather, proximity to the ocean, and relative tax-friendliness for retirees. Most areas of Delaware are affordable, although real estate in popular beach destinations such as Rehoboth Beach and Bethany Beach is extremely expensive. You should also consider whether you want to live in an area that is inundated with vacationers during the summer and somewhat deserted during the winter.

Lewes, a short drive north of Rehoboth Beach, has become popular with retirees and is more affordable.

In the north end of the state, Wilmington feels rather industrial, but several suburbs are worth checking out. These include Brandywine (surprisingly, Delaware's largest city), Newark, and Middletown.

Maryland

Maryland is a beautiful state with many distinct regions. The suburbs of Washington, DC are highly livable, but expensive. Baltimore and its surroundings offer a more working-class environment, with plenty to do around the harbor. The southeastern portion of the state that borders the Chesapeake Bay on both sides offers water recreation and laid-back small towns. The western counties, wedged between West Virginia and Pennsylvania, offer beautiful mountains and forests with cold snowy winters, although the area is chronically economically depressed.

But wherever you go in Maryland, you can't escape a high tax bill. Still, there are many desirable places to live in Maryland. I lived in Montgomery County, north of Washington, DC, for over three years and enjoyed it.

Frederick is situated in lovely green rolling hills. With a population over 70,000, it's large enough to meet your day-to-day needs. It's close enough to the DC area and Baltimore that you can drive there when you want to experience the big city, but far enough away to offer lower real estate prices and lower crime.

In the Baltimore area, check out Towson, a suburb on the north side.

If you want to live closer to Washington, DC, try the suburbs to the northeast, such as College Park, Beltsville, or other towns between DC and Baltimore.

New Jersey

New Jersey is a high-tax, high cost of living state. Property taxes are the highest in the nation.

Interestingly, New Jersey has an unusually high number of 55+ active adult communities, despite that state's smaller size, high costs, and colder weather.

If you want to live in New Jersey, there are beautiful areas in the central and western part of the state.

New York

New York is a high tax state, particularly with regard to property taxes. Since real estate is extremely expensive in the greater New York City area, in addition to high cost of living in other regards, the whole New York City area is out of bounds to all but the most affluent retirees.

If you go north to the Albany area, you'll find more affordable housing and an overall cost of living that is only slightly above the national average. The Big Apple is still close enough for occasional visits.

Cities and towns in upstate New York can be much more affordable, although they experience harsh winters.

Ithaca is about average for housing, very low on crime, and has beautiful scenic waterfalls, gorges, and the Finger Lakes for exploring and recreation. It's home to Cornell University.

Rochester, Buffalo, and Syracuse offer very affordable housing but with somewhat higher crime. The Milken Institute rates Rochester highly for good senior care, and the prestigious Eastman School of Music adds to the musical culture of the area. Milken also recommends Syracuse for walkability, outdoor recreation, and good medical services and special needs transportation.

Pennsylvania

If you're hoping to retire in the northeastern part of the United States, Pennsylvania is more affordable than most of the rest of the mid-Atlantic and New England states. The tax burden is lighter than most of the other states in this region, but it's still a mixed bag. Income tax rates are low, and Social Security and many other forms of retirement income are not taxed. State-wide sales tax is 6 percent. However, property taxes are high and Pennsylvania has one of the highest gasoline taxes in the nation.

Many areas of Pennsylvania are quite affordable, but they are also remote. The economy is still sluggish in many parts of the state, and the percentage of people living in poverty is high in many places. The nicer suburbs surrounding Philadelphia are expensive. So, finding the right mix of affordability, amenities, and desirable surroundings might be a challenge. Since most of Pennsylvania is mountainous, you can expect cold, snowy winters.

Pittsburgh may be Pennsylvania's best option as a place to live and retire. Much has been written about Pittsburgh's resurgence, as it has moved beyond a coal and steel-based economy into more sustainable sectors such as education, research, healthcare, and financial services. Pittsburgh has sufficient cultural offerings, sports teams, and Carnegie Mellon and Pitt Universities.

State College, home to Penn State, is another option to consider. It is very affordable, safe, has all the advantages of a college town, plus proximity to several beautiful state parks and state forests. However, it is remote. The nearest larger city, Harrisburg, is an hour and a half away.

If you prefer a small town, New Hope (on the eastern edge of Pennsylvania) offers a sophisticated array of antique shops, art galleries, charming restaurants, and the Bucks County Playhouse. Nearby, there are wineries, hiking trails, and historic sites. House prices are a little high, but cost of living is about average.

Washington, DC

Washington, DC is a fascinating place. Aside from the political shenanigans, it offers world-class museums, culture, history, diversity, good mass transit, and beautiful surroundings. Areas of the city vary widely, but anyplace you would probably want to live is very expensive.

The cost of living in most of DC is prohibitive for all but the most well-heeled retirees. Most parts of Montgomery County, Maryland, and Arlington, Alexandria, and Fairfax County, Virginia are, too. For semi-affordable retirement living in the DC area, you will probably need to look at least 30 miles out of town.

Southeast

It should come as no surprise that the southeastern states are popular choices for retirement. Almost all places offer low costs and mild climates. Most areas still get snow, but winters are not harsh.

There are larger cities scattered throughout the southeast, but many towns are smaller and some are quite remote.

Some remote areas experience medical services shortages. Some small hospitals have closed, leaving residents an hour or more away from the nearest hospital.

Since taxes are generally low through this region, funding for public services, infrastructure, education, and culture are often lower. These are all factors to consider, depending on your criteria.

As a general rule, I would caution you about living close to the Atlantic and Gulf Coasts due to hurricanes and nor'easters, which have increased in frequency and severity in recent years. Many coastal areas are also popular with tourists, which may impact your enjoyment of the area.

Alabama

Though not quite as inexpensive as its neighbor Mississippi, Alabama offers low taxes, low real estate, and low cost of living. Alabama is one of the poorest states in the nation and regularly ranks among the lowest for education spending.

If you are a golf enthusiast, you will find plenty of championship-level golf courses to challenge you.

Georgia

Atlanta and neighboring DeKalb County offer a cosmopolitan environment with plenty of art, music, and culture. There's a bustling bar and restaurant scene and community groups for all interests. If your retirement plans include travel, the huge Hartsfield-Jackson airport offers direct flights to hundreds of domestic and international destinations.

Aside from Augusta and Savannah, most of the rest of Georgia is rural.

Kentucky

The Blue Grass State is an excellent choice for economical living. Both real estate and cost of living are among the cheapest in the country, and taxes are reasonable. Real estate tax is especially low, and people over 65 can get a homestead exemption on $34,000 worth of assessed value. Temperatures closely mirror national averages throughout most of the state, while rain and humidity are slightly higher.

Louisville has much to offer beyond the annual Kentucky Derby. Museum Row on Main Street downtown features ten attractions within four blocks, including history, sports, art, and science museums, and several theatres. The Kentucky Center for the Arts offers traveling Broadway shows, opera, ballet, and orchestra. Louisville also has abundant green space and a large network of walking and biking pathways. While Kentucky is a mostly red state, Louisville leans Democratic.

Lexington is well-known not only for its horse farms but also for the University of Kentucky. UK hosts the Osher Lifelong Learning Institute, so retirees can take a variety of classes, participate in theatre, and use the university's fitness center. The revitalized downtown area has arts, local restaurants, and craft breweries. Real estate is slightly high by Kentucky standards, but quite reasonable compared to national averages. Lexington is politically even.

In western Kentucky, Murray is a small town of 19,000 that offers a nice mix of college town culture with excellent outdoor recreation opportunities. Murray State University is located there, and the town has a growing restaurant, gallery, and boutique scene. There are plenty of activities and clubs aimed at retirees, as well as a 'Gown and Town' initiative to connect the college with the community. Just a few miles to the east are Kentucky Lake and Lake Barkley, two long, narrow lakes which surround the Land Between the Lakes National Recreation Area.

Fun trivia: Kentucky produces 95 percent of the nation's bourbon. There are about 7.5 million barrels of aging bourbon in Kentucky, compared to 4.4 million people. Ironically, Kentucky still has 15 completely dry counties and many more counties with some restrictions on the sale of alcohol.

Mississippi

Cost of living and real estate in Mississippi are among the lowest in the nation. It's a very tax-friendly state; there is no state income tax on qualified retirement income, including Social Security. Mississippi is actively attempting to attract retirees. They have a Certified Retirement Community Program that lists 21 cities that meet their criteria. Some of the smaller cities and towns are charming.

Jackson is rated highly in the Milken Institute's study for good medical care and livability.

Mississippi is one of the poorest states in the nation and regularly ranks among the lowest for education spending.

North Carolina

North Carolina is a popular retirement choice, especially for retirees from the northeast. In fact, many people who end up retiring in North Carolina, South Carolina, and Virginia tried Florida first, didn't care for it, then moved halfway back to one of these states.

North Carolina offers a lot of diversity in various regards. The topography and weather patterns change from the coastal areas through the central piedmont to the western mountains. The larger cities all lean Democratic, while the rural areas and smaller towns are more Republican. The cost of living and real estate is close to national averages in the larger cities, and a bit cheaper in the smaller town areas. Taxation is about average.

Asheville is often mentioned in Best Places to Retire lists for its charm, culture, artsiness, and beautiful mountain surroundings. Outdoors, you can enjoy canoeing, hiking, bird watching, and mountain biking. Book lovers will enjoy perusing the extensive new and used offerings at Downtown Books and News and Battery Park Book Exchange. The city has roughly 500 restaurants and the River Arts District with over 150 studios and galleries. Houses and cost of living are a bit higher than most of North Carolina, but it's probably worth it. Winters are mild and weather patterns closely mirror US averages.

Durham-Chapel Hill is a beautiful, green area with mild winters. It's home to major universities (Duke and North Carolina) and nearby Research Triangle Park, which attracts a higher-educated, cultured population and provides a robust economic environment. Its hospitals are among the nation's best and overall medical care is very good. Cary, a smaller town between Raleigh, Durham, and Chapel Hill is nice, too.

South Carolina

South Carolina is one of the most popular states for retirement. In addition to the mild climate, it has beautiful beaches and plenty of charming historic towns. It's a low-cost state, with the exception of Charleston and Hilton Head. It's also very politically conservative, which could be a plus or minus for you.

There are plenty of retirement communities in South Carolina, with more being built. Many are being built along the coast, both for the beaches and because the flatter land is more conducive to golf courses. If you like golfing, Myrtle Beach is a golfer's paradise.

Columbia is the blue island in this red state, and is also more age-diverse than many of the places that are frequently mentioned on retirement websites. It has a nice mix of arts, restaurants, and a university community.

Charleston is undoubtably charming and historic, but also a bit pricey. Nearby Summerville is often named as a great retirement city.

The Greenville area is also worth checking out, especially if you prefer proximity to the mountains.

Tennessee

Like most of the other southern states, Tennessee has moderate but humid climate, low cost of living, inexpensive real estate, and one of the lowest tax burdens in the nation.

Unfortunately, the four major cities all have high crime rates and most of the small cities don't have much to offer. Your best option might be to find a suburb or a smaller town within a half hour of one of the larger cities. Of course, that's all in the eye of the beholder and it depends on what sort of activities you want to engage in to enjoy your retirement.

If you are a country music fan, you know that Nashville is the country music capital of the world. Otherwise, Chattanooga might be the best option. Like many cities, it has a rejuvenated downtown and the city has a nice arts scene, some good museums, an aquarium, and more. The city is bike-friendly and has good medical facilities.

Virginia

Virginia is a beautiful state with mild weather, and cost factors that are all about average. Real estate is very expensive and overall cost of living is higher in the Northern Virginia suburbs of Washington, DC, and slightly high in some of the other cities.

There are several distinct regions in Virginia.

Northern Virginia is a beautiful, vibrant, and very enjoyable area with plenty to see and do, both locally and in nearby Washington, DC and Maryland. It's also prohibitively expensive and traffic can be a nightmare. You will probably need to look in the outermost ring of suburbs 30 or more miles outside of DC to find a home that is affordable for most retirees' budgets. That might be worth it if you plan to head into DC only occasionally.

In the southeast corner of Virginia, you'll find Virginia Beach, Norfolk, Chesapeake, Newport News, Hampton, Portsmouth, and Suffolk, which are seven of the largest eleven cities in Virginia. One and a half million people live in this corner of the state. Prices are much more manageable here.

Richmond has a thriving arts scene, and is a popular filming location for movies. It is rich with colonial, Civil War, and literary history.

The western area of Virginia is beautiful with its gentle rolling hills leading up to the Appalachian Mountains. If this area appeals to you, check out Charlottesville or Blacksburg, both college towns (Virginia and Virginia Tech, respectively) with reasonable prices and low crime.

Note that Virginia has a personal property tax, so you will pay taxes on your car, boat, or RV every year.

West Virginia

The best (and perhaps only) reasons you might consider moving to West Virginia are that it's very cheap to live there and the mountains are beautiful. Tax-wise, it's not particularly favorable and the state taxes Social Security. But house prices and other costs of living are low enough to offset the somewhat higher taxes.

Mining has long been one of the main drivers of West Virginia's economy, so many areas of the state have been economically depressed for a long time and will probably remain so.

If you want to live in West Virginia, consider Morgantown. Thanks to the presence of the University of West Virginia, the area is more stable and prosperous, there are more options for culture and entertainment, and crime is very low.

Florida

Florida has been the #1 retirement destination state for decades, and that should remain the case for years to come. Most people are drawn to Florida for its warm weather and very light tax burden.

Not surprisingly, there are more 55+ active adult communities in Florida than anywhere else. 55Places.com lists 415 of them, and that's not counting RV/mobile home parks. I will discuss the pros and cons of active adult communities in another section of this book.

Real estate in the southeast area of the state (the Keys, Miami, Fort Lauderdale, Boca Raton) is expensive, but throughout most of the rest of the state, it's cheap.

Florida has its downsides. It is hot and very humid in the summer. Orlando and the beaches receive a lot of tourist traffic. Florida has some beautiful areas, but there are many areas that aren't particularly attractive. In the areas with a higher concentration of retirees, some people complain about high traffic during the winter season and seemingly endless generic-looking strip shopping centers and chain restaurants.

Florida is popular with snowbirds, so areas that are popular with retirees may be packed during the winter months and deserted during the summer months.

Personally, my biggest concern with Florida is hurricanes. Within the past decade, hurricanes have struck nearly every part of the state. The east coast and the Panhandle seem to be the most vulnerable, so if hurricanes are a concern, you may fare better on the central Gulf Coast or inland.

Orlando may be best known for Disney World, Universal Studios, Sea World, and other tourist attractions, but there is much more to Orlando than just its theme parks. Those are located outside of Orlando anyway.

Orlando has several popular gentrified neighborhoods such as Thornton Park, Lake Eola Heights, and Colonialtown. The cost of living, house prices, and tax rates are particularly low in Orlando. And if you are hoping to receive plenty of visits from your family and friends after you retire, the proximity to the ubiquitous theme parks can't hurt.

Tampa and nearby St. Petersburg offer larger-city amenities at a very affordable cost. The Ybor City neighborhood in Tampa, a National Historic Landmark District, offers entertainment and night life. St. Petersburg is home to some world-class museums and a growing art scene.

For what it's worth, Orlando is WalletHub's top choice for Best Retirement City in 2019,[11] followed by Tampa at #2.

Miami and Fort Lauderdale both suffer from high real estate prices and high crime. If you want to live in that area, consider Pembroke Pines – it's much safer, and while real estate is more expensive than some parts of Florida, it's more affordable than Miami and Fort Lauderdale.

Midwest

Illinois

Illinois residents suffer from high taxes across all categories – high real estate taxes, a flat-rate income tax of 4.95 percent, and sales tax of 8.64 percent. Illinois has been financially mismanaged and has the lowest credit rating in the nation.

At least the cost of living is lower, and almost all retirement income is not taxed. There are some property tax breaks available for seniors.

If you want to live near Chicago, consider the more affordable and safer suburbs of Aurora and Joliet.

Away from Chicago, Champaign is very affordable and offers the benefit of being a university community.

If you are looking for a small town with lots of charm and interesting things to do, check out Galena, in the northwest corner of Illinois. It's downtown looks like a throwback to the 19th century when the town was home to Ulysses S. Grant. Now, there are 125 shops, galleries, and restaurants to discover, along with a handful of distilleries, microbreweries, and wineries. Crime and cost of living are remarkably low. For bigger city needs, Dubuque, Iowa is just over 15 miles away.

---

[11] https://wallethub.com/edu/best-places-to-retire/6165/

Indiana

Indiana is about average in terms of tax burden, but the cost of living and the cost of real estate are among the lowest in the country. It's very affordable.

Bloomington is home to Indiana University, with one of the best music schools in the country as well as the newly expanded Sidney and Lois Eskenazi Museum of Art. For outdoor lovers, Lake Monroe and Brown County State Park are nearby. Real estate is slightly high by Indiana standards, but lower than US averages. It's sufficiently safe and cost of living is low. Bloomington is about 50 miles away from Indianapolis.

About 37 miles east of Bloomington lies Columbus, one of the most unique and remarkable cities you'll find anywhere, especially if you appreciate interesting architecture. It has six buildings designated as national historic landmarks and dozens of other buildings designed by world-renown architects. Outdoor recreation is available nearby at Lake Monroe and Brown County State Park, and Columbus has an excellent symphony orchestra. Columbus is located about an hour south of Indianapolis, an hour and 15 minutes north of Louisville, and two hours west of Cincinnati.

Indianapolis itself is very affordable, although some parts of town may be less safe.

Iowa

One of the most notable impressions of Iowa is presidential primaries. It's true that this state offers you the best chance to meet and hear candidates than anywhere else. Iowa has earned its reputation as a political bellwether thanks to its politically balanced population. The cities mentioned here lean slightly Democratic, although the balances are close. Rural areas of the state lean more Republican.

Iowa is a good state for retirement for other reasons. Across the state, cost of living and real estate is low, crime is low, and taxes are better than average. The state's population is well-educated and its diversified economy should keep it in good shape. As with many Midwest and farm belt states, winters are windy and cold, while summers can get very hot and humid. The state is also subject to tornadoes and thunderstorms. If you don't mind the temperature extremes, or if you plan to become a snowbird, Iowa is worth checking out.

The Des Moines/West Des Moines area offers some of the best geriatric care services in the nation that are also relatively reasonably priced. There are many libraries and recreational facilities that will make it easier to stay fit in winter weather, and community volunteerism is high. Crime in West Des Moines is lower than in Des Moines.

Iowa City is the Milken Institute's #1 small city for its excellent healthcare, good transportation, and general livability. Ames also ranks high.

Cedar Rapids and Dubuque also offer low real estate, low cost of living, average or lower crime, and a variety of things to do.

Michigan

Michigan offers a variety of retirement opportunities, all of which have one thing in common: cold winters. Many retirees live in Michigan during the summer but migrate to warmer locations during the winter.

Cost of living and cost of real estate are low. The tax burden is about average, but Michigan is phasing in some new taxes on various forms of retirement income. So, Michigan is not exactly rolling out the welcome mat for retirees.

If you enjoy water recreation, Michigan has the longest fresh water coastline in the world. That's not hard to believe since it borders four of the five Great Lakes.

Michigan offers some vibrant college towns and livable medium-sized cities. There are many small, charming lakeside communities up and down the coasts as well, offering beautiful lake views and a relaxed pace.

Traverse City, with just over 15,000 people, is one of the larger cities on the northern stretch of the Lake Michigan coastline. There are many other small towns, lakes, rivers, biking trails, sand dunes, and other points of interest within reach. I once saw Traverse City mentioned on a Top Ten list of best foodie cities in the country.

On the other side of the state, Midland is a charming city which owes its prosperity to the presence of the headquarters of Dow Chemical company. Midland has that 'Main Street USA' feel to it. It's not far from the larger Saginaw and Saginaw Bay, an offshoot from Lake Huron.

Ann Arbor is all about the University of Michigan; its presence is a dominating influence in the city. As a result, there's not much of a focus on seniors, but the residents tend to be highly educated, there are plenty of cultural offerings, and healthcare is excellent.

The towns of Saugatuck and Douglas, on the 'art coast' of Lake Michigan, have a combined year-round population of about 2,000. But these towns can swell to three times that size during the summer season. Saugatuck's Oval Beach has been named one of the top 25 beaches in the world by Conde Nast and the nearby sand dunes are visually stunning. Between the two towns, there are a wide array of shops, galleries, restaurants and lodging options. While Saugatuck and Douglas thrive during the summer months, winters are cold and annual snowfall is over six feet. Median house prices are approximately $300,000, which makes this area a relatively expensive choice. Nearby Holland, famous for its massive tulip gardens, has more reasonable house prices. For more even year-round living with less tourism and lower prices, Grand Rapids is just 40 miles away.

Minnesota

Minnesota is a high-tax state, and it gets very cold in winter.

Minneapolis and St. Paul offer a high quality of life, but with higher than average cost of living and real estate to match. Of the two, St. Paul is more affordable and safer. Nearby Bloomington has lower crime and slightly lower real estate prices.

The Milken Institute ranks Minneapolis-St. Paul-Bloomington highly for good transit with special needs support, highly educated population, good healthcare, and plenty of things to do.

Missouri

Missouri offers low cost of living and low real estate, especially outside of the larger cities. It's weather patterns closely mirror US averages and taxes are about average.

Columbia frequently shows up on Best Places to Live and Best Places to Retire lists, for a variety of good reasons. Cost of living is low, crime is low, and real estate is about average. It's home to the University of Missouri, Columbia College, and a number of smaller schools. It has plentiful cultural offerings, good economic health, and excellent healthcare.

Kansas City offers a great music scene, famous barbeque, and low prices, but unfortunately that's offset by high crime.

Ohio

If you don't mind cold winters and humid summers, Ohio has a lot to offer retired people. The cost of living is below the national average and cost of real estate is among the cheapest in the nation. Taxes overall are slightly higher than the national average, due primarily to sales tax. Income tax rates are reasonable and Social Security is not taxed. Ohio has no estate or inheritance taxes.

The six largest cities – Columbus, Cleveland, Cincinnati, Toledo, Akron, and Dayton – all offer a nice blend of culture, sports, and activities. All six of these cities scored 100 on the Human Rights Campaign's Municipal Equality Index.[12] Ohio has many charming smaller towns with colleges and universities.

Home to one of the largest universities in the country and numerous corporate headquarters, Columbus is well-educated, open-minded, and cultured. German Village, just south of downtown, is quaint neighborhood with charming old brick homes, while the Short North area just north of downtown is home to numerous galleries. Columbus has a thriving jazz scene, and there are plenty of music and theatre performances offered at Ohio State and downtown. The winters can be harsh, but the low cost of living and real estate make the area easily affordable.

Columbus is rapidly growing, while the other five cities are shrinking. Columbus offers the best choices for living within city limits; in the other five, you'll find better options in the suburbs due to high crime rates in the cities.

Toledo is rated highly by the Milken Institute for good transit for older adults, good quality healthcare, and plentiful recreation options.

---

[12] https://www.hrc.org/mei

Wisconsin

Wisconsin has high property and income tax, but Social Security and military pensions are not taxed.

Madison is a very pleasant, livable, and affordable city. It's home to both the state capital and the University of Wisconsin. Madison offers good medical services. Many hospitals have geriatric, Alzheimer's, and rehab units, and emergency room waits are generally short. The city is safe and very walkable, and there are plenty of fitness centers and outdoor opportunities.

Great Plains

Kansas

Kansas is not particularly tax friendly, but cost of living and real estate is low in much of the state.

If you want to retire in Kansas, Lawrence is a good choice. It's highly rated by the Milken Institute for good healthcare. It's home to the University of Kansas and is the cultural center for the area. Real estate prices and crime rates are reasonable, and overall cost of living is low. At just under 100,000 people, it's a medium-sized city, but it's just 30 minutes from Topeka, 45 minutes from Kansas City and Overland Park, and an hour from the Kansas City International Airport. Nearby Clinton Lake offers recreational options. Politically, Lawrence leans left in an otherwise very Republican state.

Nebraska

Nebraska is a fairly high tax state, especially compared to its neighboring states. However, cost of living is low, so the tax bite might be easier to handle. Property tax as a percent of home value is high, but real estate is not expensive. Social Security and pension income are taxed, and income tax rates are high.

Omaha is an inexpensive place to live, and healthcare is excellent. There are numerous fitness centers, recreational opportunities, and libraries. Community volunteerism is high. Politically, it's pretty even. Crime is slightly high, though.

Council Bluffs, Iowa is just across the river, so you might find a more advantageous tax environment there. Otherwise, the cities are very similar.

North Dakota

North Dakota is not particularly tax-friendly, and it taxes Social Security. It's the third least-populated state in the nation with about 750,000 residents. There's a lot of wide-open, remote spaces. North Dakota is semi-arid, but also subject to cold winters, high winds, thunderstorms, and blizzards.

On the plus side, North Dakota has a strong economy due to oil.

Fargo, the state's largest city located on the Minnesota border, seems like the best choice. It has a good cultural scene and the cleanest air in the country. The Milken Institute ranks Fargo highly for good healthcare, strong economy, and community engagement. Cost of living is slightly above national averages, but still affordable.

South Dakota

The best feature about sparsely-populated South Dakota is that it's tax friendly. It has no state income tax, low sales tax, and reasonable property taxes. Cost of living is low, too.

Sioux Falls, South Dakota's largest city at around 180,000, is highly rated by WalletHub and Milken for good healthcare, high funding for independent senior living, and strong local economy. It's safe and affordable, although somewhat isolated. It's a four-hour drive to Minneapolis-St. Paul.

South-Central

Arkansas

The best things you can say about Arkansas are that it's affordable and it has plenty of beautiful lakes, hills, and the Ozark mountains. The tax burden isn't particularly favorable, but with such low cost of living it may not matter.

If you are interested in planned retirement communities, Arkansas has some large ones.

Arkansas is not generally known as a cultural hotspot, but if you're looking at Arkansas, you may want to look at Fayetteville and Bentonville in the northwest corner of the state.

Eureka Springs is an artsy, touristy town in northwest Arkansas. The town boomed in the late 1800s as a resort, and much of the era's Victorian architecture has been preserved. The entire town is listed on the National Register of Historic Places. Boating, hiking, hunting, and fishing are all within easy access, as is Fayetteville, home to the University of Arkansas. Eureka Springs is somewhat of a liberal oasis, in stark contrast to most of the surrounding area.

Louisiana

Louisiana is promoting itself heavily as a retirement destination. It has a Certified Retirement Community Program which includes many communities large and small. Louisiana is a low-tax, low cost of living state. Winters are mild, but the state receives a lot of rain and humidity from the Gulf of Mexico.

New Orleans is famous for its French-quarter charm and its bohemian entertainment, but real estate and crime are relatively high and it is susceptible to severe hurricane damage. It's a fun place to visit, but may not a great choice for a place to live.

Similarly, you may wish to avoid other areas that are near the Gulf Coast due to the potential for hurricanes.

Further inland, there are many nice towns. The larger cities are relatively higher-priced and higher-crime. There are some charming smaller towns that may offer the amenities and ambiance you're looking for.

Oklahoma

With low cost of living, low house prices, and low taxes, Oklahoma is worth considering if living cheaply is a priority for you in retirement. Oklahoma's terrain varies as you move across the state, from lakes and mountains in the east to flatter, more open spaces as you move west.

Oklahoma has one of the highest Native American populations, with 50 tribes in the state.

Oklahoma winters are mild and summers are hot and humid. Oklahoma experiences higher than average winds and tornados, and some other natural disasters such as flooding and fires. In recent years, some areas of Oklahoma have experienced an increase in mild tremors, which have been attributed to fracking.

Oklahoma is politically conservative.

Tulsa is an attractive city with plenty of lakes and parks and some good cultural offerings. If you are drawn to this area, consider the suburb of Broken Arrow – crime is significantly lower there.

One other city of interest is Bartlesville, about 45 miles north of Tulsa. Bartlesville is home to many Conoco Oil executives, the only Frank Lloyd Wright-designed skyscraper, and the massive Bartlesville Community Center which offers much more art and entertainment than you would expect in a city of 36,000.

Texas

Texas is one of the most popular retirement destination states due to its warm climate and low cost of living. Texas has no state income tax and therefore no taxes on retirement income. Sales tax is higher than average, and property tax rates are among the highest in the nation.

Cost of real estate varies widely. Generally, it's low, but there are some very expensive areas in each of the major metro areas. Each of the major cities (Houston, San Antonio, Dallas, Austin, Fort Worth, and El Paso) has its own personality and offers a wide variety of options, especially when you consider the surrounding suburbs as well as the cities themselves.

Winters are generally mild, but many parts of Texas can get snow and ice in the winter. Summers are very hot and often humid, with occasional heavy rains. Areas close to the Gulf Coast are susceptible to hurricanes.

Austin is a diverse, liberal oasis in an otherwise politically conservative state. The city is home to the state government, the University of Texas, and many high-tech and pharmaceutical companies. Austin is famous for its live music scene, with more music venues per capita than any other US city. Austin is one of the most rapidly growing cities in the country. Many residents hope to preserve the city's quirky and artsy culture with the motto, "Keep Austin Weird."

Healthcare is excellent, and nursing homes and in-home care is relatively inexpensive. Real estate prices are reasonable (but not cheap), and overall cost of living is slightly below the US average. Crime is about average. Suburbs such as Round Rock may offer slightly lower costs and crime rates. Since Austin has been consistently appearing on Best Places to Live lists for a long time, the city will continue to attract people and real estate prices may go up in the future.

Texas has many small towns and medium-sized cities too. Some are driven by the oil economy and some have become popular choices for retirement. If smaller cities are more to your liking, I recommend staying within an hour's drive of a larger city so you can still avail yourself of the healthcare, shopping, and other support amenities. Some areas of Texas are quite remote.

Texas has a Certified Retirement Community Program which identifies places that have the services, amenities, and other desirable factors for good retirement living.

Southwest

Arizona

For years, Arizona has been the second most popular retirement destination, after Florida. It's also popular with snowbirds from the western half of the US and Canada.

Phoenix (more specifically, its southeastern suburbs) has been my home since 1995. I was born and raised in Ohio, lived in the Washington, DC suburbs for over 11 years, then moved to the Phoenix area in my late 30s. I had grown tired of cold, snowy winters and heavy traffic, and I was ready for a change. Plus, I saw that I could own a house for half the cost of Northern Virginia or Montgomery County, Maryland, and other prices were lower too. Cost of living, real estate, and taxes are all fairly close to national averages.

At the time I moved, I wasn't even thinking about retirement destinations, I just wanted to live someplace warm, sunny, and affordable. Phoenix delivered on all counts. 24 years have passed and I'm now retired, and I still love living here.

Yes, it gets very hot in the summer. As the cliché goes, "but it's a dry heat!" Temperatures between 100°F and 110°F, when coupled with 20-30 percent humidity, are warm but not unbearable. When it gets over 110°F at times in July and August, there's no denying that it's really hot. So, we stay inside where it's air-conditioned or enjoy our pool. Sometimes, when it's 110°F outside and I'm floating in the pool sipping a Mojito, I remember what it was like to shovel a foot of snow and scrape ice off my windshield in Ohio's 10-degree weather. I'll take the heat any day. You don't have to shovel sunshine.

If you aren't familiar with Arizona, it isn't one big desert. It is quite geographically diverse and there are many distinctly different climates in Arizona. About a half-hour north of Phoenix, the elevation suddenly increases about 2,000 feet at the Mogollon Rim, and that high desert region enjoys temperatures that are at least 20 degrees cooler, with winters that are cold enough to receive snow. As elevations rise in the northern and eastern parts of the state, you'll find pine trees, much more rain, and snowy winters. You might be surprised to learn that there are at least three ski resorts in Arizona.

Still, the majority of Arizona's 7 million people are concentrated in its two largest metro areas, Phoenix (4 million) and Tucson (700,000). With the exception of #2 Tucson, the top 11 cities in Arizona are Phoenix and its suburbs, collectively called the "Valley of the Sun."

The Phoenix metro area's plentiful 55+ active adult communities are spread around the outskirts of town. The larger ones include Sun City, Sun City West, and Sun City Grand to the northwest, Pebble Creek in the west end, Sun Lakes to the south, and Leisure World in Mesa. If you want to live closer to the heart of the city, you might prefer some of Phoenix's well-preserved historic neighborhoods just north of downtown or the suburbs of Tempe, Chandler, Gilbert, or Ahwatukee. For the lowest real estate prices, look in the Sun Cities or east Mesa/Apache Junction.

Phoenix has grown rapidly over the past several decades, along with its foodie scene and many cultural offerings. Winters are delightful, but you'll want to have access to a pool to enjoy the hot summers.

Tucson, about 100 miles southeast of Phoenix, is actually 5-10 degrees cooler than Phoenix. Tucson has a good arts and culture scene, and real estate is inexpensive. Parts of Tucson have somewhat high crime numbers, but if you look in the northern part of the city, the northern suburbs of Oro Valley and Marana, or Vail to the southeast, you'll find low crime and very pleasant surroundings.

Green Valley, a particularly appealing 55+ community, is located 20 minutes south of Tucson.

Prescott and Prescott Valley, about 100 miles north of Phoenix, are popular with retirees. This area offers all four seasons as well as nearby lakes and mountains for outdoor recreation.

Pinetop-Lakeside and Show Low are well-developed resort-like communities in the higher elevations, about 3 1/2 hours northeast of Phoenix. Many people have weekend homes here, but others live year-round. The area is large enough to offer most amenities you'll need, including golf courses, a ski slope, a hospital, and a nice variety of locally-owned, non-chain restaurants.

Nevada

Nevada is an excellent option for retirement. It is among the states with the lowest total tax burdens in the nation. There's no income tax, no estate or inheritance tax, property taxes are low, and sales tax is only slightly high. Cost of living and cost of real estate are quite affordable in most of the state.

In the southern end of the state, which includes Las Vegas and the surrounding cities, it's sunny, warm, and dry, with very little rainfall or snow. Temperatures are about 5-10 degrees cooler than Phoenix. Near Reno, the state's other population center, it's also sunny and dry, but cooler. Summer highs reach 90°F, while winter lows dip into the 20s. Reno gets snow in the winter.

Both of these areas are popular choices for retirees.

In Las Vegas, there is plenty to do apart from 'The Strip.' The suburbs south of Las Vegas, such as Paradise, Enterprise, Henderson, and Spring Valley, offer lower house prices and lower crime than Las Vegas itself. There are many retirement communities here. This is one of the fastest-growing areas in the country.

Reno and nearby Sparks are close to numerous lakes such as Lake Tahoe and a lengthy stretch of mountains and national forests.

Mesquite is a relatively new city about 80 miles northeast of Las Vegas, located along I-15 near the Arizona and Utah borders. It offers milder weather, lots of 55+ communities, and plenty of golf courses and other outdoor activities. Its biggest drawback is its remoteness.

New Mexico

Retirement options and their price tags vary widely in New Mexico. New Mexico is only somewhat tax friendly. Social Security is taxed, but most of their other tax rates are reasonable. Outside of Santa Fe, the cost of living in most of the state is pretty low, so taxes may not be a major consideration.

The jewel of the state is its capital, Santa Fe. At 400 years old, it is the United States' oldest capital city. It is historic yet modern. Its vibrant downtown area is home to interesting museums, outstanding restaurants, and dozens of galleries. Santa Fe is a charming, delightful, very livable city. Of course, because it's so desirable, houses are quite expensive. Due to its elevation, winters are cold. Like most of the state, it's dry with lower-than-average rainfall and snowfall.

Albuquerque, by far the state's largest city, is less expensive. You'll find plenty of good restaurants offering authentic New Mexico cuisine. Choose your neighborhood carefully, though; Albuquerque, as a whole, has a high crime rate, but some areas are fine.

Las Cruces, near the state's southern border, offers somewhat warmer temperatures and only occasional snow, although winter low temperatures still dip into the 20s. Real estate is inexpensive and crime is about average. At first glance, Las Cruces might seem sleepy and laid-back, but there is plenty of culture to enjoy and beautiful mountains surround the city. It's about 45 minutes to El Paso, so you won't be too far from big city amenities and a good airport when you need them.

Much of New Mexico is depressed – both economically and otherwise. Education levels are low and many people are poor. In the Land of Enchantment, the landscape can be easily shift from beautiful to desolate. I suppose enchantment is in the eye of the beholder.

Rocky Mountains

Colorado

Colorado is among the more tax-friendly states in the nation.

If you enjoy the mountains for hiking, skiing, or breath-taking beauty, the Denver area is hard to beat. Real estate in Denver itself is a bit pricey, so you may wish to venture into the suburbs. Denver also offers highly-rated medical care, a prosperous economy, and well-funded transit for elderly adults. Denver rates high for overall quality of life and its residents are among the healthiest and most physically active in the country.

Silver Sage Village, in the suburb of Boulder, is one of the United States' first cohousing communities.

Fort Collins, about an hour to the north, is less expensive and offers many of the same qualities as Denver but on a smaller scale. It's also home to Colorado State University.

Grand Junction, near the Utah border, is also worth consideration, especially if you love the mountains and outdoor activities. Year-round temperatures closely mirror the US averages, but it's sunnier, less humid, and windier than average. While this is a large enough city for most needs, it's four hours to Denver and almost five hours to Salt Lake City. Colorado Mesa University, with 10,000 students, offers Lifelong Learning and a Golden Scholars Program. Cost of living is below average but crime is a little above average.

Idaho

Idaho is a popular state for retirement. In one recent study, it was among the top ten states that retirees are moving to. If you like lots of sun and low rainfall, low humidity, outdoor activities, and close access to rivers and mountains, this might be the place for you. Temperatures vary widely across seasons; Idaho can get quite hot in the summer and very cold in the winter.

Taxes are about average, and cost of living is lower than average. Real estate prices vary, but are generally reasonable.

Boise, the state capital, is frequently mentioned on Best Places to Retire lists. It's a large enough metro area to offer plenty of culture and things to do, yet it is affordable and not too large. Boise is the easternmost city in a metro area that also includes Meridian, Nampa, Caldwell, and numerous smaller suburbs. Boise seems to offer the best value, with Meridian being a little more expensive. Nampa and Caldwell don't appear to be quite as appealing.

Further east, Pocatello is worth consideration. Real estate is very inexpensive and crime is below average. Winters are colder and snowier than in Boise, but summers are also hot, sunny, and dry with little rain. Pocatello is home to Boise State University, which offers a lifelong learning program called New Knowledge Adventures, in which people 50 and older can take unlimited classes for a reasonable fee.

Coeur d'Alene, located farther north in the Idaho panhandle, offers affordable living with beautiful mountain scenery and several nearby lakes. Spokane, Washington, is about 30 miles away, so between the two cities there are plenty of options to keep you engaged.

Montana

Montana offers spectacular scenery and great outdoor adventure. Summers are sunny, dry, and pleasant, but winters are harsh. Many areas of Montana are designated as national forests or Indian reservations. Glacier National Park is here, along with the northern edge of Yellowstone. With so many remote, sparsely populated areas, the nation's fourth largest state has just 1.1 million residents. With an average age of almost 40, Montana is also one of the nation's oldest states.

Montana has no sales tax, but it taxes Social Security and most other retirement income. Cost of living is below average, but real estate prices in Montana are higher than you might expect in many areas of the state, especially near tourist resort towns and in Bozeman. Ranch land is in demand with wealthy people, which has driven prices up.

Billings is the state's largest city, with a population of about 110,000. It combines an Old West ambiance with that of a modern city with a healthy economy. There are dozens of buildings on the National Register of Historic Places, but plenty of modern facilities like a large performing arts center, museums, a zoo, and a good hospital system. The Heritage Trails System offers miles of hiking and the city is bike-friendly.

Missoula, the state's second largest city with 70,000 people, is home to the University of Montana, which offers a lifelong learning program. The city is sometimes referred to as the 'Left Bank of Montana,' due not only to its location near the western border but also its progressive bent. It offers arts festivals, free summer concerts, art galleries, and the

Montana Lyric Opera. Nestled in the mountains, it also offers plenty of fishing, hiking, biking, and skiing nearby.

Utah

Utah is the fourth fastest-growing state in the country, thanks to its robust economy. Consequently, real estate has become expensive in parts of the state, particularly the Salt Lake City area and the popular ski towns such as Park City and Deer Valley. Utah is home to five spectacular national parks and Monument Valley, with its often-photographed sandstone formations.

Most Utah cities, while not necessarily cheap, are very livable. They have low unemployment and are very bike-friendly. Not surprisingly, most of Utah is conservative and about two-thirds of its residents are members of the Church of Jesus Christ of Latter-day Saints (Mormons). Eighty percent of the state's residents live in the string of cities from Provo to Ogden along I-15, with the Wasatch Mountains to the east and Great Salt Lake to the west.

It may seem surprising that Salt Lake City, home to the world headquarters of the Mormon Church, is actually quite diverse and progressive. Winters are cold, but there is world-class skiing nearby as well as the famous Sundance Film Festival in nearby Park City. Medical care is highly rated, with ample geriatric, rehabilitation, physical therapy, and memory care services. If you plan to do some work during your retirement years, SLC has strong 65+ employment levels.

If you are a golf enthusiast, St. George, in the southwest corner of the state, is a golfer's paradise. With year-round sunshine, low humidity, and low amounts of rain and snow, the climate more closely resembles that of Las Vegas, which at 120 miles away is the closest big city. St. George is very politically conservative.

Moab, a small, isolated town of 5,000 in eastern Utah, is situated between the Arches and Canyonlands National Parks, both renowned for their stunning natural beauty. The area thrives on outdoor adventure and is popular with mountain bikers, hikers, and whitewater rafters, so it can get crowded with tourists. Moab is a bit more liberal than most of the rest of Utah. Downtown Moab offers an interesting array of foodie restaurants, art galleries, and shops. It has art walks, music festivals, and a week-long Pride festival. Since Moab is situated in an arid high desert region, it experiences chilly winters and warm summers with light annual precipitation and snowfall. The nearest large city, Salt Lake City, is over 230 miles away. Grand Junction, Colorado, is 113 miles away.

Wyoming

Wyoming is the least populated state in the country, with less than 600,000 residents. It is extremely tax-friendly, with no income tax and low sales tax. Wyoming collects most of its money from property taxes, the 7th highest in the nation.

Like Montana, Idaho, and northern Utah, it's dry and sunny, with warm summers and frigid winters.

In most areas of Wyoming, the population is very sparse and you would be pretty far from anything. Cheyenne, in the southeast corner of the state, is about 100 miles north of Denver.

Cheyenne and Casper are Wyoming's two largest cities, each with a population of approximately 60,000. House prices are about average, but cost of living is low. They are also very safe.

Northwest

Oregon

In recent years, Oregon has placed among the top ten states that retirees are moving to. This is especially impressive since it's not a sunbelt state and the west coast is rainy. Though it's not as sunny and warm, the climate is nevertheless very pleasant – it never gets too hot or too cold. Between the coastline, the mountains, and the Columbia River valley, the state is filled with natural beauty and recreational opportunities.

The price of all this quality of life and popularity is that real estate prices are high and rising, especially in the Portland area.

Oregon has no sales tax, but income tax is among the highest in the nation. Social Security is not taxed, fortunately. Property tax rates are about average, but with property values soaring, you could end up paying more property tax in the future.

In the past couple decades, Portland has become one of the trendiest destinations in the US, both for the Millennial generation and for the

LGBT community. Portland has mild winters and beautiful summers, but it's rainy throughout most of the year. Portland has expensive real estate, so a more economical option would be to settle across the Columbia River in Vancouver, Washington, where the median house price is significantly lower. This option allows you to live in Washington, where there is no state income tax, and shop in Oregon, where there is no sales tax.

Salem, the state's capital, offers cost of living, real estate prices, and crime that are all about average. Eugene and Corvallis, home to Oregon's two major universities, are slightly higher but offer all the cultural benefits of college towns. Corvallis is safer, too.

Bend, located closer to the center of the state, is popular with outdoor enthusiasts, and has been growing in popularity with retirees. Real estate prices are growing too, but cost of living is average and crime is low. Bend gets considerably less rain than the cities listed above.

Washington

Washington offers beautiful scenery and a pleasant climate, although it's rainy in much of the west. Washington has no income tax; therefore, Social Security and other forms of retirement income are not taxed either. The state makes up for this with somewhat higher than average property and sales taxes.

The string of cities from Olympia and Tacoma to Seattle and Bellevue offers many good choices for beautiful places to live with lots to see and do. Of course, the closer you get to Seattle, the more expensive real estate becomes. Everett and Olympia are somewhat more affordable. Prices are lower in other areas of the state.

In eastern Washington, check out Walla Walla. The city of 33,000 is sunny and dry, although still chilly and snowy in winter. It's close to the mountains and the Columbia River. With over 100 wineries in the region, it has been nicknamed 'the Napa of the North.' There are several breweries and distilleries as well. The cost of living and real estate is considerably cheaper than the cities in western Washington.

Spokane, the largest city in eastern Washington, is pleasant in many ways. It boasts 75 parks and 76 nearby lakes, the surroundings are beautiful, and it offers a sufficient amount of culture and activities.

Coeur d'Alene, Idaho, another nice city, is 30 miles away. Cost of living and real estate are reasonable, but crime is high.

Sequim (pronounced "skwim"), on the Olympic peninsula, offers beautiful scenery and recreation with its proximity to both the Olympic mountains and Puget Sound. The city of 7,000 has a unique characteristic: while most of the Pacific northwest is often cloudy and rainy, Sequim receives noticeably less rain than anywhere else in the region. Pilots flying into Seattle noticed there was usually a hole in the clouds above Sequim, due to its position in relation to the mountain range. The nearest larger city is Port Angeles (19,000), from which you can take a ferry to Victoria, British Columbia. However, it's a 1 hour, 45-minute drive to Tacoma and a 2 1/2-hour drive to Seattle, including a ferry ride.

Alaska

Alaska is probably not going to make it onto your list of retirement possibilities unless you really love winter and you don't have to be too concerned with affordability. Practically everything costs more in Alaska because so many products have to be shipped in.

On the plus side, Alaska has the lowest tax burden of any state in the nation. There's no state sales tax (although some municipalities charge it), no income tax, no inheritance tax, and only 24 municipalities levy property tax.

The state has traditionally received almost all of its income from oil and gas production, but that has been slipping in recent years, causing the state to grapple with diversifying its revenue stream.

Alaska actually pays residents to live there. Each year, the state pays each resident a dividend from the Alaska Permanent Fund, which is funded by oil revenue. In recent years the dividend has slipped from $2,000 per person to $1,000 as the state has needed to tap the fund for operating revenue.

Alaska's population is around 750,000, but population has been rising steadily for the past seven decades.

Anchorage is the only city of any size in the state, and its crime rate is high.

Sitka, a small town in the Alaska panhandle, is charming and offers some cultural interest and outdoor recreation. Real estate is expensive, but crime is low.

With any town in the panhandle, be aware that this is region is cloudy and rainy for most of the year.

California

In the 60s, the Beach Boys sang of surfing, sunshine, and California girls and Tony Bennett left his heart in San Francisco. Add in the glamour of Beverly Hills, the intrigue of Hollywood, the magic of Disneyland, and the year-round warm, sunny weather, and California became the go-to destination for anyone seeking a better, sunnier life. It was America's land of milk and honey. People flocked there in droves. Metropolises exploded, prices soared, and freeways clogged.

There's no question that California offers a lot: beaches, entertainment, mountains, deserts, forests, wine regions, and exciting cities. Many places in California still possess an undeniable coolness factor. The climate in most of the state is wonderful. You'll probably never run out of things to see and do.

It should come as no surprise, then, that most of California is very expensive. In the major metro areas, real estate is exorbitant. Couple that with a fairly high property tax rate, and you'll be paying a lot of property tax.

Income tax is high, too. A couple earning about $60,000 will pay 6 percent state income tax. The highest marginal income tax rate is 13.3%, the highest in the nation. Pension income is taxed, but Social Security is not.

Gasoline is about a dollar a gallon more than anywhere else.

On top of that, California is more susceptible than many states to natural disasters such as earthquakes, extreme droughts, and forest fires. The Los Angeles area is infamous for its smog and nightmarish traffic. Traffic can be pretty bad in San Diego and the Bay Area, too, but at least the Bay Area has good mass transit.

If you hope to live in any of the three major metro areas, you will need a lot of money to put a roof over your head or be willing to live in a very small, modest dwelling.

If you like the San Francisco Bay Area, you may have to live as far away as Sacramento to find real estate prices that might be affordable by the standards most of the rest of the country is accustomed to.

In Los Angeles and San Diego, there are some outlying suburbs that may work. In the San Diego area, consider Chula Vista. For Los Angeles, you may find yourself in the Palm Springs area instead. Rancho Mirage and Palm Desert have relatively affordable prices.

In the northern part of the state, you might consider medium-sized towns like Eureka or Redding. They are cheaper, cooler, greener, and offer a more relaxed pace. However, this may not be what you have in mind when you envision living in California. You can find similar surroundings in other states with lower taxes.

Hawaii

If you have ever been to Hawaii, you have no doubt been captivated by the beauty of the mountains and the sea shore, the lovely weather, and the overall sense of casual ease and serenity. It is truly the embodiment of a tropical paradise.

At some point during your stay, you probably fantasized about what it might be like to live in such a beautiful place. Maybe you have entertained the idea of retiring to Hawaii.

For me, those fantasies were quashed as soon as I walked into a grocery store and saw prices that were at least double the cost of groceries at home. Similarly, a quick perusal of real estate prices convinced me that Hawaii is well outside of the affordable range for us and for many other retirees.

During our trip to Hawaii, we took a cruise ship tour that visited Kona and Hilo on the big island, Maui, and Kauai. On two different islands, our tour guide told us the same story.

They each said that people visit Hawaii, fall in love with it, and then move there – either when they retire or perhaps while they are still working. They usually last about six months, then they move back to the mainland.

They return because they miss their family or they get bored, or both.

Both tour guides claimed that, outside of Honolulu, there is not much to do. Everything closes up at 5 p.m..

When you experience Hawaii as a tourist, you're probably staying in a fancy hotel or a vacation condo on Waikiki Beach or any of the beach towns that dot the perimeter of Maui, Kauai, or the big island. You spend your days on the beach, exploring the island, and eating and drinking in the tourist-oriented restaurants and bars.

Like most vacations, it's a welcome change of pace from your job and your day-to-day life.

But if you live in Hawaii full-time, your home probably won't be right on the beach. You won't spend every day on the beach. You won't be eating, drinking, and partying with the tourists. Before too long, you'll probably prefer to avoid the tourists and the tourist areas.

After the novelty of living in Hawaii wears off and you get into your new daily routine, what will you do?

In the Honolulu metro area, where over 950,000 people live (two-thirds of Hawaii's total population), there are sufficient non-tourist options to keep the local people engaged. Elsewhere, not so much.

Real estate and cost of living are cheapest in Hilo, relatively speaking. However, Hilo experiences high rainfall and only 40 percent sunshine. Monthly precipitation averages range from 8 inches in June to 17 inches in November. This is probably not the Hawaii you're dreaming about.

Property tax in Hawaii is quite low, given the high cost of real estate. Sales tax is 4 percent, although local cities may add more. Income tax is high, though, making Hawaii not particularly tax-friendly.

You should also consider that returning to the continental US to visit family and friends will involve a long flight. It's 5 hours and 40 minutes from Honolulu to Los Angeles.

PART FOUR

Is a 55+ Active Adult Community Right for You?

Chapter 10

The Retirement Community Phenomenon

On January 1, 1960, an event occurred which would dramatically alter the concept of retirement in the United States, and to a lesser extent, other areas of the world.

On the date, real estate developer Delbert Eugene Webb opened a new residential development in a sparsely populated area about 15 miles northwest of downtown Phoenix, Arizona, along US 60. The new development, called Sun City, opened with five model homes, a shopping center, a recreation center, and a golf course.

Despite it being a holiday, Webb boldly predicted that 10,000 people would come to see his new model homes during the opening weekend.

This estimate was especially optimistic, because this community was not targeted for the overall population. Only those aged 55 and older would be able to buy houses in this new development.

At the time, there was only one other planned community in the nation that was limited to residents age 55 and above. That was Youngtown, located just to the south, which was launched in 1954. Youngtown was probably an inspiration to Del Webb, who was approaching 60 at the time. But Youngtown was small, and was primarily just a housing development.

Webb envisioned something much grander: a community where residents could enjoy golf, tennis, shuffleboard, swimming, social events, and clubs – all in an environment dedicated exclusively to retired people.

Webb wasn't just selling houses; he was selling an exciting new lifestyle filled with carefree recreation, new friends, and fun.

As it turned out, Webb was wildly incorrect. The opening weekend didn't draw 10,000 people. It drew over 100,000 people. Try to imagine 100,000 people descending upon five small model homes in one weekend!

The overwhelming success of the Sun City launch resulted in a *Time* magazine cover story, a priceless promotional boost that further fueled the demand for this new vision of retirement living.

Between 1960 and 1975, Sun City grew to over 29,000 housing units in 14.5 square miles, with a population of over 40,000. The population has been gradually decreasing since its peak in 1980.

When Sun City filled up, Webb began building Sun City West, a few miles to the northwest. By the time it was built out in 1998, another 15,000 homes had been built in 11 square miles. Population peaked at 26,000 in 2000. Next, Webb built Sun City Grand, and his company is now building Sun City Festival. Del Webb has also built active adult communities in California, Nevada, New Mexico, Texas, Tennessee, North Carolina, South Carolina, Georgia, Virginia, Indiana, Michigan, New Jersey, Connecticut, and of course Florida.

Del Webb is hardly the only developer of these communities. Today active adult communities can be found in every state. They range from luxurious high-end country club-like resorts with professionally designed golf courses to mobile home and RV parks with no amenities at all. There's a community for every budget and lifestyle.

Exact data are difficult to find and the numbers are changing constantly. As of mid-2019, there are about 2,400 active adult house communities in the United States. Add in 55+ mobile home and RV parks, and the number swells to over 4,000.

There are several websites you can consult to help you discover the options for active adult communities in whatever areas you are interested in. My favorite is TopRetirements.com. That website covers the entire spectrum of communities, including some outside the United States. It has information about most cities and towns, so it's useful for people who are researching places to live in general, not just in retirement communities. It has a state guide for every state and several foreign countries that contains useful information such as climate, real estate prices, and taxes. It has a 'Retirement Ranger' search tool where you can enter criteria that you're looking for in a retirement destination and it will return a list of areas that match your requirements. Finally, the website posts a new article each week to its blog, and it has an engaged subscriber base that always provides interesting perspectives in the comment forum.

Another good website is 55places.com. This website focuses only on active adult communities, not mobile home and RV parks and not general information about cities and towns. However, they have a 70-person staff who researches each community in order to provide unbiased information, and they do not accept money from developers or communities to help promote them. For each community, they link to a real estate agent who has been vetted for quality and expertise. They have a blog with thousands of articles on every imaginable topic related to living in 55+ active adult communities.

Chapter 11

Changing Retirement Trends

Several factors suggest that the concept of the 55+ active adult community may be losing favor with those who are entering retirement now and those who will be retiring during the coming decades.

1. Diversity

Over the past few decades, the United States became increasingly diverse. This trend is driven by the increase in immigration, particularly from India, China, Mexico, and the Middle East. LGBT people are now living their lives more openly, and the amount of religious diversity has increased as well.

These demographic shifts have already taken place in most of corporate America and academia. People who work in these environments have become accustomed to working with diverse people, and many have come to appreciate the rich and interesting experiences that come from being surrounded by different people.

Unfortunately, the demographics of this country's 55+ active adult communities are not changing as rapidly. Most people who appreciate living among diverse people are going to be less interested in retiring to a community that still looks very white, straight, Christian, and conservative.

Of course, there's nothing wrong with any of these attributes. It's just that the number of people with different characteristics has increased significantly.

While many of the current residents of these retirement communities may have no problem with seeing more diversity among their neighbors, that may not happen until we pass a tipping point where there are enough diverse people living in a community to shed its homogeneous image.

In other words, the perception that 55+ active adult communities are overwhelmingly white, straight, Christian, and conservative will discourage people of other demographics from moving into these communities, so these communities will remain overwhelmingly white, straight, Christian, and conservative. It's a self-fulfilling prophesy.

While there are a few communities that cater to various minority populations, such as LGBT people or Jewish people, this approach won't solve the problem, either. A growing number of future retirees want diverse communities. These specialty communities may provide a sense of safety and homogeneity for those of a particular demographic, but they are equally non-diverse.

2. Recreational shifts

The choice of recreational activities is gradually shifting as the Baby Boomer generation heads into retirement. A recent study by the Physical Activity Council[13] revealed some interesting findings.

Activities that are increasing in popularity include camping, bicycling, hiking, and canoeing. Activities that are decreasing in popularity include golf, swimming for fitness, and working out using machines or weights. These shifts have ramifications for active adult communities with regard to the amenities that they have traditionally provided for their residents.

While some shifts may be attributable to how strenuous the activity is, others appear to rise or fall depending on the cost to participate.

As these recreational shifts play out, active adult communities that feature golf courses may become less desirable as future retirees choose where to live. Golf courses are expensive to maintain, and re-purposing

---

[13] http://www.physicalactivitycouncil.com/pdfs/current.pdf

the land would be costly and probably objectionable to current residents. It could become harder for current residents (or the executors of their estates) to sell their homes to future buyers.

Another interesting finding is that physical activity tends to increase based upon one's income. This is probably due to the fact that many sporting activities require money to purchase clothing and gear and pay for the costs of participation, such as gym memberships and greens fees. If retirees feel squeezed by inflated healthcare costs or insufficient savings, they have less money available for physical activities.

Today's retirees are spending more time using technology, engaging in creative pursuits, or continuing to work, and this impacts how much time those retirees spend engaging in recreational activities.

3. Generational Changes

Where retirement is concerned, everyone is focusing on the Baby Boomers – those born between 1946 and 1964.

However, it's useful to take a look at the previous generations and how the concept of retirement has changed, and will continue to change, across generations.

The Greatest Generation – those born between 1901 and 1924 – experienced the Great Depression and World War II. They were finally able to settle down into normal lives in the late 40s, 50s, and 60s.

Next came the Silent Generation – those born between 1924 and 1945. This is the generation that entered adulthood starting at the end of World War II and whose working careers spanned the 50s, 60s, 70s, and 80s.

While it's always risky to characterize entire generations of people with broad brush strokes, it seems clear many people in these two generations thrived on conformity. Men were more likely to stay with a company for their entire career and women were more likely to be stay-at-home wives and mothers. Gender roles and social norms were firmly entrenched. In the earlier years, racial segregation was common in both institutional and social structures. LGBT people were invisible, never spoken about, and widely discriminated against, since they were so firmly outside of the prevailing gender roles and social norms.

People's lives were tightly scripted in terms of going to college, finding a job, getting married, raising a family (primarily the woman's domain), following a career path with a single employer (primarily the man's domain), and retiring with a pension and Social Security.

When Sun City, Arizona arrived on the scene on January 1, 1960, the Greatest Generation was ready to start retiring, and after the hardships of their earlier lives, they were ready to play. Retirement meant ceasing work altogether. For those who could afford it, it meant golf, tennis, shuffleboard, and perhaps traveling in a trailer or motorhome.

The Baby Boomers are different. They grew up in the 60s and 70s, listened to rock and roll, smoked pot, protested the Vietnam war, and rebelled against the boundaries of music, clothing, hair styles, sexual mores, gender norms, and discrimination. People changed jobs, changed careers, and changed partners. It was the generation of women's liberation, two-career couples, civil rights, and the start of gays and lesbians coming out.

Individual Retirement Accounts (IRAs) and 401(K)s were introduced and pensions started disappearing.

Where previous generations thrived on conformity, the Baby Boomers thrive on individuality. The Baby Boomer generation is more independent, educated, and free-thinking. They seek personal growth, gratification, affluence, and purpose. They probably changed employers or careers several times and most people no longer rely on a pension.

This is playing out as the Baby Boomers retire. More and more Baby Boomers are choosing not to follow the traditional retirement script. Fewer Baby Boomers want golf courses and tennis courts. More want creative outlets such as art, music, and writing to express their individuality. They can indulge these passions now that they don't need to rely on them to produce income.

In retirement, they are less likely to opt for slowing down and kicking back. Many will continue to work in some form or another, either out of necessity or by choice. Many want to still contribute to society.

Are 55+ active adult communities losing their appeal?

Most of these communities are located on the outskirts of cities or in rural areas. Many people who are retiring now and in the next 5-10 years are more likely to want to stay in the mainstream of society and live closer to an urban center than to retreat to a retirement village.

Many Baby Boomers don't want to putt around their self-contained community on a golf cart. They value walkability, bike lanes, and good public transportation. They want access to good foodie restaurants and local culture.

All of these generational changes portend a shift away from the gated, master-planned, 55+ active adult communities with amenities galore and high home owner's association (HOA) fees to match. Baby Boomers don't want to pay for golf courses and other amenities they won't use.

If you are considering moving to one of these communities, especially a larger one, I highly recommend that you read *Leisureville: Adventures in America's Retirement Utopias*, by Andrew D. Blechman. (This book was retitled *Leisureville: Adventures in a World Without Children* for the paperback and Kindle editions.)

The copyright date on this book is 2008, which means the data quoted in the book are over ten years old now. At that time, active adult housing was the fastest growing sector of the housing market.

However, back then there were already signs that the demand might be abating, even though an estimated 10,000 people turn 65 every day.

According to a generational marketing expert quoted in the book, people from pre-Boomer generations (and perhaps the earlier Boomers) valued conformity and community. They viewed retirement as a time to just kick back, play, and party after a long work career. Many of the people Blechman interviewed at The Villages in Florida expressed a keen desire to live with no children around. They flocked to communities such as The Villages and Sun City.

Today's Boomers (at least the latter half of the generation born in 1946-1964) and those who will follow want anything but a giant one-size-fits-all age-segregated, planned community. They want homes that meet their unique needs, a more 'authentic' lifestyle experience, and to be closer to families and friends.

People entering retirement today want purpose and fulfillment. They are more adventurous and individualistic. Today's retirees are more likely to be starting businesses, pursuing creative passions, and exploring the world.

And just as the people entering retirement today rebelled against the 'establishment' in the late 60s and early 70s, they are now rebelling against the old notions of what retirement should look like – including moving to age-segregated communities.

Today's retirees don't even think of themselves as being older. I know I don't.

Of course, this is how I feel at age 62. When I'm 75, I might feel very differently. And as active adult communities evolve over the next 10-15 years, perhaps they will embrace the desires and the diverse demographics of today's and tomorrow's retirees.

The Industry is Responding

Some developers have noticed the decrease in demand for golf courses. Some communities that are currently being developed are changing the mix of amenities being offered. For example, developments near water may have kayaks or stand-up paddleboards for residents. Some may offer bicycle rentals and repairs, or trendy restaurants with demonstration kitchens.

At some communities, less than 20 percent of the residents are golfers. Golf is dwindling in popularity among younger Baby Boomers and subsequent generations, but even those who played golf in their younger years are too busy with other pursuits to have time for golf. Rather than devote a large amount of land to a golf course that will be expensive to maintain and underutilized, some new communities are building golf simulators. The golfer will hit a real golf ball on a real tee, but the simulator can offer up to 300 different courses to play on.

Developments with larger amounts of land available are now more likely to use that acreage for hiking and biking trails, equestrian facilities, vineyards, and gardens.

Research has shown that among opposite-sex couples, women more often drive the decision to move to a 55+ active adult community, and they are often more socially oriented than their husbands. To address this trend, some new developments are building man caves to lure the men out of their homes to socialize. These man caves include billiards, darts, poker tables, and large-screen TVs for watching sports. Some women like them, too.

The bottom line is that the range of amenities being offered is broader than ever. If you are considering moving to an active adult community, it's important for you to consider what activities will appeal to you.

Chapter 12

12 Factors You Must Consider Before Moving to a 55+ Retirement Community

Active adult communities have been immensely popular choices with retirees for several decades.

Many people are drawn by the appeal of living in a safe, leisure-focused environment that is isolated from many of life's realities, such as rush-hour traffic jams, undesirable neighborhoods, and families with children.

While the lifestyle and amenities that age-restricted active adult communities offer are a good fit for many retirees, these places are not for everybody. If you are considering moving to a retirement community, here are twelve questions you must consider before you put your house on the market and start packing.

1. Will you enjoy living in a self-contained community?

Most retirement developments are located on the outer edges of cities or in rural areas. If most of the activities and entertainment options you hope to enjoy are offered on-site, this won't be a problem.

But if you plan to attend concerts and theatre, visit museums, dine in a wide variety of restaurants, and avail yourself of many of the other amenities a medium or large city has to offer, the drive into town may be too long. Also consider whether your shopping needs can be met on-site or within a reasonable distance.

2. Will you prefer to be surrounded by other retirees or would you rather stay in the mainstream?

This is a highly personal choice, and there's no wrong answer. Arguably, surrounding yourself with people of different ages will keep you better connected with what's going on in the world and can enable you to stay younger at heart.

3. Will you fit in?

When you visit potential communities that you may retire to, notice the demographic characteristics of the residents. Many communities tend to be homogenous with regard to race, religion, political views, and socio-economic class.

For example, The Villages in central Florida, the largest and fastest-growing active adult community, is over 98 percent white and politically very conservative.

If you are a minority, try to determine if there are other residents like you and how welcoming the residents seem to be towards diverse people.

Most retirement communities, especially those in Florida and other southeastern states, are overwhelmingly conservative. If you consider yourself liberal, how well will you fit in with a community where the majority of residents hold opposing views? While you may prefer that politics not often enter into the realm of everyday life, it will sooner or later, especially during election cycles. How well will you deal with social situations when the conversation turns to politics and most others have viewpoints that are different from yours?

One person who rented a home in a 55+ community commented on an article on RetireFabulously.com, "We have always been very active volunteers in the cities we have lived in and we like to choose when and where we socialize. There seems to be an unwritten rule here that you need to participate in their structured activities or you will be considered unfriendly."

4. Is the community well maintained?

The overall appearance of the community and the first impression you get can tell you a lot about how well the community is being run and whether they have sufficient operating funds to keep up with maintenance.

5. What are the rules, and can you live with them?

Almost all planned retirement communities are governed by a homeowner's association (HOA). The HOA has rules which apply to many aspects of your residential experience, such as what pets you can own, how you can decorate the exterior of your home, and how long younger guests may visit. In some communities, these rules are quite far-reaching and restrictive. Ask for a copy of the Covenants, Conditions & Restrictions (CC&Rs) and read them thoroughly.

If you are part of a couple in which one of you is older than 55 and the other is younger, almost all communities will permit the younger partner to live there. But what happens if the older partner dies? Will the under-55 survivor be allowed to stay, or must he or she sell and move out? Check the CC&Rs and ask if you're unsure.

6. How much is the HOA fee, and what does it cover?

The monthly fee you pay to live in a community may be high, but a lot depends on what you will get for your money. The HOA fee includes your share of the cost of common area maintenance, the community's employees, insurance, and property taxes, to name a few.

Find out what other services the fee covers, such as utilities, trash collection, cable, and Internet. Will you be paying for amenities and services you won't use? For example, if you are not a golfer, you may not want to live in a community that features golf courses that are maintained with everyone's monthly fees.

In larger retirement communities, there may be multiple levels of fees. For example, in some areas of Sun City, Arizona, residents pay into mini-HOAs that cover the landscaping of their immediate area while also paying into the city-wide organization that maintains the rec centers and other public amenities.

Also be aware that sometimes fees have different names. For example, in Sun City, Arizona, real estate listings claim that there are no HOA fees. However, residents pay about $500 per year to maintain all the recreation centers and finance their activities.

7. Who owns the amenities?

While a community is still being built, the amenities such as the activity center and the golf course are usually owned by the developer. When the development reaches a certain percentage of completion, ownership will transfer to the HOA. Try to learn whether this transfer has taken place and, if not, whether the process is clearly defined in writing. This can be a tricky and potentially contentious period in the life of a retirement community.

Is the HOA board is comprised of residents or people who are affiliated with the developer? This information is particularly important if the developer still owns the amenities. When the time comes for the developer to sell the amenities to the HOA, then if the HOA board is packed with the developer's operatives, the residents could easily be overcharged for these assets. It has happened, including at The Villages in Florida.

8. Is the HOA in good financial shape and well managed?

Ask to see the HOA's financial statements for the past year or two. You can determine whether the HOA has a good budget and how well they perform to the budget. Items to look for include whether the HOA maintains sufficient reserve funds, whether and how often they impose assessments, and whether they have a problem with delinquent payments from residents. If the community has a lot of vacancies and foreclosures, those homeowners probably aren't paying their fees and the financial health of the HOA will suffer.

Also try to determine how much HOA fees have increased in past years.

Ask to see the minutes from HOA meetings for at least the past year, as well as other communications from the HOA board and the community's staff to the residents, such as newsletters or a website.

You can assess the general health of the community from these documents. You can tell whether the HOA board is running the community in a disciplined, responsible manner or if they are constantly dealing with complaints and problems. You can assess whether the general tone of communication is upbeat or whether residents are frequently being admonished with reminders of what they cannot do.

9. What clubs and planned activities are available?

Some communities have dozens or even hundreds of clubs for residents to join, connecting people who share just about any common interest imaginable. If these clubs are officially chartered, they may receive a budget that comes from the HOA or recreational fees you pay.

Try to find out what sorts of organized activities the rec center offers. These may be anything from aerobics classes to holiday parties.

Earlier in this book, I stressed the importance of visualizing what you want your life to look like after you retire and what sorts of activities you want to be able to enjoy. When you evaluate a 55+ active adult community, consider how well the community's offerings align with how you want to spend your retirement. Think about whether you are likely to participate in these organized activities or whether you are more inclined to manage your recreation and social life independently.

Some residents have reported being ostracized if they don't participate in at least some clubs or activities.

10. Are your prospective neighbors happy?

Talk to several people who live in each retirement community you are considering. Ask them what they like most about living there and what they would improve. Try to determine whether they are happy with how the community is being operated and if they have any complaints. Ask if they get along well with their neighbors.

11. Will you have sufficient privacy?

In most active adult communities, houses are placed close together and there are usually no walls or fences between the houses. Occasionally, a community may have low half-walls separating lots which make it easier to distinguish property boundaries but still offer no privacy.

The intent of this design is probably to create a feeling of openness, unity, and connection.

This may be fine for you, or it may not. You may enjoy seeing and being seen by your neighbors so you can wave and enjoy a few moments of chit-chat. This design also makes it easier for neighbors to watch each other's houses when people are away.

But some of your neighbors might be nosy and you may prefer not to have others watching everything you do.

12. What is the mix of year-round residents and part-time residents?

In some active adult communities, a significant percentage of the homes are owned by snowbirds. This will mean that the level of participation in various clubs and activities will vary significantly throughout the year. Your community may be hopping during the winter months and boring during the summer months. If you plan to live there year-round, how will this impact you?

This factor could make it more difficult for merchants and restaurants in the area to operate year-round.

Moving to any new place is a multi-faceted decision. Moving to an age-restricted active adult community introduces several additional lifestyle and financial factors that are probably different from anywhere you have lived before. It pays to do your due diligence and gather as much information as you can before you make this significant investment.

When visiting a community you are considering retiring to, take an official tour with either a sales representative from the community or a realtor. You will receive a lot of information that it would be impossible to obtain just by driving through or searching online. Of course, you'll get a sales pitch, too. Then spend some time away from the sales rep or realtor and talk to people individually.

Some communities that are still building may offer 'stay and play' visits in which you can briefly experience what it's like to live there. In other cases, rental units may be available.

This process can easily take many months or even one or two years. Take the time. Don't just buy into the first place that looks good enough or the place that sweeps you off your feet on your first visit.

Chapter 13

Sun City Revisited

Before we leave the topic of 55+ active adult communities, let's check in with Sun City, Arizona today. Sun City is now 60, which means that it is older than some of the people who are currently moving there.

Sun City looks dated. The appearance factor is probably more pronounced in the Phoenix area than it would be in many parts of the country, because house styles have changed dramatically in Phoenix suburbia over the past 60 years. Today, modern homes have stucco walls and Spanish roof tiles. In Sun City, most homes are brick – often light-colored brick or brick that has been painted white – with shingle roofs. Some have design features that are long out of date. Worst of all, some people have painted the landscape rocks in their front yard green. It's unspeakably tacky.

The newer parts of Sun City West do not look quite as dated.

Some homes have been remodeled, but some have not. I have toured a few homes that were for sale, and I have visited a few others during the course of my business as a wedding officiant. Unless the homes have been remodeled, the kitchen cabinets and countertops, bathroom fixtures, closets, and light fixtures look very dated and are often in poor condition.

Prices for homes in Sun City and Sun City West are among the cheapest homes in the Phoenix metro area on a price-per-square-foot basis. They are a bargain, since the area is safe to live in. They tend to stay on the market longer than usual, because they are only available to buyers who are over 55 years old. Besides, if you are in the market for a home in a 55+ active adult community in the Phoenix area, you are probably going to be less inclined to buy a 50- or 60-year-old house that looks out of date and is in need of renovation when you can buy a house in one of the shiny, modern new developments being built in the area.

That said, everyone I have asked who lives in Sun City says they like it. One of my friends who admits that he moved there primarily for financial reasons says he likes it better than he thought he would.

The reason I mention this is so that you will consider what it might be like to sell your home in any of the current retirement communities in 20 or 30 years. Newer communities will have been built during the ensuing years. As the Baby Boomer generation grows older and the smaller Gen-X generation starts retiring, there will be fewer buyers. If current demographic trends continue, fewer of them will be inclined to live in an age-restricted community far away from an urban center.

If you live in your home until you die, you probably won't be much concerned about resale value. But at some point, if you need to sell your home and move into a continuing care or assisted living facility, you may not have as much equity in your home to assist with that expense as you might need. And it may be difficult to wait several months for your home to sell to gain access to that money.

It's something to think about.

PART FIVE

Other Considerations

Chapter 14

The Case for Staying in Place

While it's fun to imagine what it would be like to live in some of the interesting, exotic, and less expensive places mentioned in this book, many people don't actually follow through.

Just as there are good reasons to move after you retire, there are also compelling reasons to stay right where you are. You may love your current home and have a strong emotional connection to it. Perhaps you want to remain close to your network of family, friends, and support systems rather than start over with making new friends, learning a new area, and finding new doctors and other service providers. If you are planning to start a business, you will need the network you have built up over many years. Sometimes moving is not financially feasible. Or perhaps it boils down to inertia and it's easiest just to stay put.

If you want to remain in your current home for the rest of your life, here are several considerations that will help you decide whether this is the best choice for you.

1. Does your current community have good infrastructure for supporting seniors?

This includes good public transportation or perhaps the availability of city-sponsored transport vans, good healthcare, and a strong senior center that provides activities as well as support services.

You should also consider whether you live close enough to public transportation and whether the places you visit regularly are on transportation routes. Now that services such as Lyft and Uber are available almost everywhere, public transportation may not be nearly as important.

2. Is your house adaptable to meet your needs as you grow older?

A one-story floor plan, or at least a floor plan with a bedroom and all necessary facilities on the first floor, will make it easier if you should require a walker or wheelchair during your later years. Other adjustments might need to be made, such as replacing door knobs with lever handles, adding ramps, and retrofitting your bathroom with handrails. If you or your spouse should someday require a wheelchair, you should evaluate whether doorways are wide enough and if countertops, cabinets, closets, and bathroom facilities will still be accessible.

3. Are your house and yard easy enough to maintain as you age?

This concern can be managed if you have nearby family members who are willing to assist you or you can afford to hire people to help you with cleaning and maintenance. Keep in mind that family members may move.

4. Is your current house in good condition and energy efficient?

Depending on your house's age and condition, you may incur costs to repair or replace an aging furnace, air conditioner, carpet, appliances, or roof. Occasional home maintenance tasks such as repainting or removing dead plants may become things you can no longer do yourself.

If you are concerned about finances, these unplanned expenditures may have an impact on your budget.

5. Are most things you need available within a reasonable distance?

Driving all over town and maneuvering on crowded freeways will become more challenging as you get older.

6. Are the amenities you wish to enjoy during retirement close by?

While you worked, you were probably most concerned with living a reasonable distance from your workplace. After you retire, your work commute will be replaced by trips to play sports, take classes, hike, and participate in other activities that you select to be part of your retirement lifestyle.

7. Will your neighborhood still be safe?

As you get older, safety will become an increasing concern. While it is impossible to know what transformations your area of town may undergo in the coming years, you may be able to assess whether your surroundings are improving, holding steady, or declining based on unemployment rate trends, population trends, and the health of local businesses.

8. Does your area have good assisted living or nursing homes that you would want to live in?

It may be decades before you need them, and a lot may change over the course of those years. When you reach the age where you will need to move into such a facility, your search will probably be limited to your current area. Try to determine whether your local facilities are pleasant and affordable for you and whether there is a long waiting list for spaces.

After considering all of these questions, you may still conclude that remaining in your home is the right choice for you. Hopefully this chapter has called attention to steps you can take now in order to ensure that your home will continue to serve you well as your needs change.

Of course, you can remain in your current city and downsize to a smaller home. That way, you'll retain your familiarity with the area, proximity to your social and support network, and your preferred medical professionals.

If you anticipate moving locally, it will probably be to your advantage to do that sooner rather than later while you have more stamina for a move. Downsizing will probably reduce your housing costs, leaving you more money to enjoy your retirement in other ways.

Chapter 15

Is Downsizing the Right Choice for You?

Many people move to a smaller house at some point after they retire. Downsizing might make sense for both financial and logistical reasons, but it might not be an advantageous choice in every situation. There are many factors you should consider in order to decide whether downsizing is right for you.

Here are some of the pros and cons of moving to a smaller home.

Pros:

1. You will gain access to the equity in your house

A significant portion of your net worth is probably tied up in your home equity. When you trade your current house for a less expensive one, you free up that money to invest in other ways or simply to have more money to spend.

2. You may lower your monthly costs

A smaller house will probably have lower utility bills or taxes, and cost less to insure. But be aware that these costs may be higher in your new locale, even for a smaller home.

If you have equipped your current home with solar panels, a newer and more efficient air conditioner, extra insulation, or other energy-saving features, you will lose those benefits if your new home doesn't have them.

3. You will have less to maintain

A smaller house means less to clean. If your new house has a smaller yard, that will require less effort to maintain. If you move to an apartment, a condo, or a retirement community where exterior maintenance is included in your monthly fee, you will eliminate that chore altogether.

4. Downsizing will force you to reduce your possessions

You have probably accumulated a vast array of possessions over your lifetime. Tidying has become a popular craze over the past few years, but you may not feel any urgency to toss your extraneous possessions if you have no plans to move in the foreseeable future. It can be liberating to get rid of all those things you no longer use. You'll also leave fewer possessions for your heirs to sort through and dispose of after you're gone.

Cons:

1. Moving is costly

The cost of moving, disposing some of your possessions, the realtor's commission, and the money you spend to fix up and furnish your new home could easily amount to 10 percent of the cost of your current house.

2. Your house might require a lot of repairs and upgrades before you can sell it

You may be perfectly satisfied with your house's decades-old fixtures and you have learned to live with a few things that don't work as well as they should anymore. But when it comes time to put your house on the market, your realtor may suggest that walls need to be repainted and carpet needs to be replaced, and all those repairs you have put off for years now need to be made. All of this will cost money.

3. Moving is a hassle

It takes a lot of time and energy to pack and unpack. For everything you're not going to move, you will need to sell it, donate it, dispose of it, or make arrangements for your kids to come and get what they want. (Hint: they probably want a lot less of your stuff than you think.)[14]

You will also need to stop and start utilities and change your address in countless places. And while the idea of tidying may seem appealing, you may find that it's difficult to part with possessions that you have an emotional attachment to.

4. Your monthly expenses may increase

The monthly fees in retirement communities and condominiums are often substantial, and they will probably increase over time. The homeowner association or condo fee may surpass the amount of money you will save on utilities. In some condominiums, you may have to pay extra for parking or storage space.

5. Your new house could have problems of its own

If you buy a house, you could be inheriting problems that need to be fixed. Before you buy, try to find out how old the air conditioner, furnace, and hot water heater are. Make sure your home inspector does a thorough check on the roof. Ask the seller to include a one-year home warranty plan in the deal.

6. Your travel costs could increase

If you are moving far away from your family and friends, you will incur travel expenses whenever you want to visit them.

---

[14] https://www.nytimes.com/2017/08/18/your-money/aging-parents-with-lots-of-stuff-and-children-who-dont-want-it.html

7. If you are married, you may have less room for personal space

You and your spouse probably enjoy having a place to go when you want some time away from each other. This is where you go to work on your hobby, listen to music, or read. In a smaller house, there may not be room for each of you to have your own area, and you will spend more time in close proximity.

8. You may be emotionally attached to your house

Even if you determine that it would be financially beneficial for you to move to a smaller house, you may not want to go. Plus, you are familiar with your current neighbors and your surroundings, and you will have to re-orient yourself in your new locale.

Chapter 16

Should You Rent or Buy?

Throughout this book, I have repeatedly recommended that when you move to a new place, either domestically or internationally, you should rent first before you buy. This will give you time to determine whether or not you truly like a place before you commit to it. It will also allow you more time to discover the best neighborhoods and find a good realtor.

But should you buy at all?

In the United States, homeownership is a dream of most people, and we are conditioned to believe that owning your home is preferable to renting. When you own, each monthly payment builds equity. When you rent, the money simply goes into the landlord's pocket and builds equity for him or her.

If your house is paid off, monthly expenses decrease significantly because you are paying neither rent nor a mortgage payment.

But there are reasons why it might make more sense to rent when you move to a new location after you retire. A lot depends upon your financial situation and how long you think you will stay in a place. Here are several factors to consider:

If you expect to live in a place less than five years, it may be more beneficial to rent. If you buy and sell more often, the realtor's commission is more likely to negate the money you gain from the appreciation of your house (assuming it appreciates), and you'll be paying realtor's commissions and other closing costs more often. If the market drops during your short stay, you could lose even more.

When you own a home, your home equity isn't working for you. Let's say you own a $300,000 house that is paid off, or you buy a $300,000 home in your new location and pay cash for it. That $300,000 isn't invested and isn't earning any sort of interest or dividends. The value of the house may go up or down, but it will do that regardless of whether you own it outright or carry a mortgage.

Instead of buying that $300,000 house, suppose you found a place to rent for $1,500 a month. That's $18,000 a year you would be paying in rent. It would take over 16 years for your rent payments to exceed $300,000, although that doesn't factor in rent increases. In the meantime, the money could be invested and/or spent on enjoying your retirement.

Renting also offloads many maintenance expenses and obligations. It gives you more flexibility to move later on, although the older you get, the more moving becomes a challenge.

If you are moving to another country, the case for long-term renting is even stronger. The laws and taxes pertaining to homeownership are different from what you are familiar with, and owning may not be favorable for foreigners. In some countries, there are limitations on how much money you can move out of the country per year, which could become problematic when you sell. Do your research!

There are arguments to be made on both sides. The best choice depends upon your finances and other circumstances. But enter into this decision with an open mind; don't assume that buying is always the best choice.

Chapter 17

Avoid These Common Mistakes When Choosing Where to Retire

Throughout the course of researching information for this book, I have encountered numerous examples of mistakes people commonly make when choosing a place to retire. Here are some common pitfalls to avoid as you set out to find your Retirement Utopia.

1. Choosing a place because it was a good vacation experience

I have harped on this one, but it bears repeating here. Just because a location makes for a wonderful vacation doesn't mean it is a good place to be a permanent resident. Usually, it's not.

The presence of tourists will probably become an annoyance to you once you move there. Tourists drive up prices, traffic, noise, and sometimes crime.

Most vacation destinations are seasonal. The place may be dead during the off-season, and the weather may be significantly different.

2. Living someplace just to be near your family

This is a tricky one. If you have children and grandchildren, you would probably prefer to see them more rather than less. If you have aging parents, you may feel obligated to care for them, as well as wanting to spend as much time with them as you can during their final years.

All of this is fine if the place your family lives also makes a good place for you to enjoy your retirement.

But if living near your family means that you must live in an expensive place that depletes your savings too quickly, or a place that does not have good resources and services for seniors that you may need one day, or a place where you won't have access to activities and amenities that you would like to enjoy, then living near your family might not be the best choice.

Also, consider that your kids may move to follow their careers.

3. Not considering your future needs

It's easy to be short-sighted when you think about where you would like to live after you retire. It's fine to visualize your retirement being filled with golfing, going to the beach, and other leisure and recreational activities. Those are important.

But uncomfortable as it may be, you should also think about what medical services and senior support resources you'll need later on. Make sure the place you decide upon can serve you as well in ten or twenty years as it will during the first few years.

4. Not researching the total cost of living in a place

Many retirees move to another state because they can buy more house for less money. One thing they often don't look into is what the property taxes will be in the new location. Often what they save from their lower house price is eaten up by increased property taxes and other costs.

In the US, taxation varies widely by state. You can use taxfoundation.org and other websites to determine things like how much you'll have to pay when you renew your car's license tags, whether or not Social Security and pension income is taxed, and whether or not there are property tax breaks for retired people.

Figuring out how much it will cost you to live in a place is a tricky exercise with a lot of factors to take into consideration.

The cost of groceries, gasoline, alcohol, entertainment, and many other items vary widely across the country. When you are visiting a potential new place, go into stores and note the prices of products you commonly buy.

Find out what the utility rates are, and try to estimate how much electricity and/or gas you'll need to use based on the climate throughout the year. You can search online for 'utility rates in _____' and you will get results from websites like SmartAsset.com and Numbeo.com as well as discussion forums.

If you are going to live in a retirement community or any neighborhood that has an HOA, understand what fees you'll have to pay and what they cover.

If you move to a foreign country, merchandise that you buy online from another country may be subject to heavy import tariffs. You'll need to learn about how you will be taxed when you live there.

If you move to a place that is far away from your friends and family, either to another country or to another part of the same country, try to estimate how much will you spend traveling back to visit. You may end up traveling back more often than you think.

5. Failing to notice what's not there

It's easy to see all the features and advantages a place has to offer. It's not so easy to spot things you want to be part of your retired life that aren't available. That's why it's so important to think about the little things that you appreciate having in your day-to-day life.

For example, a place that has wonderful weather, great hiking trails, and beautiful surroundings may be lacking a good book store, local community theatre, and a place to get good Thai food.

What would you really miss if it wasn't there?

How far will you have to go to find things you really need?

6. Diving right in

Probably the most common mistake people make is committing to a place without spending a significant amount of time there first.

Spend as much time visiting a place before moving there as you possibly can. Visit during different seasons. Talk to local people.

Research the place thoroughly, both online and in person. Don't go there as a tourist; visit the local stores, restaurants, and other places you would go to frequently if you lived there.

Whether domestically or internationally, always rent before you buy.

PART SIX

Alternative Retirements

Chapter 18

Retiring to a Rural Area

When Cathy and Jeff retired a few years ago, they moved from Crown Point, Indiana, a city of 27,000 in northwest Indiana on the edge of the greater Chicago-Gary-Hammond metropolitan area, to a house on a lake in a rural area of southeast Indiana. The nearest towns, with populations of 11,800 and 6,500, are 15-20 minutes away.

"We chose the lake because of the peacefulness of it. Just sitting looking out at the lake brings a relief of stress. It's the best way to enjoy your morning coffee. We also wanted a place that was close to where our girls live (within an hour) and offered activities and a community.

"From where we lived in Northwest Indiana, we were an hour away from Chicago. Here we are an hour from both Cincinnati and Indianapolis. We are able to take advantage of cultural events in both areas without nearly as much traffic and congestion. We miss certain particular things about Chicago but there are opportunities here as well. We do miss many things about Crown Point. It was more developed and had a more vibrant town life than here.

"I think the biggest adjustment we've had to make is being at least 15-20 minutes from any kind of store or restaurant. There are two small restaurants out here that feature the basic burger fare. We have to go into Greensburg or to Batesville to buy groceries or gas, visit a doctor, or go to church. We now have lists of things to get while 'in town' as the trip is not a quick one.

"We need to plan our time to get anywhere, but since we are retired it's not such a stressor. Weather is milder here in the winter but we still need to be mindful of conditions as far as when roads will get cleared and possible power outages.

"However, people are very helpful. Just recently our 4-wheel drive vehicle got caught in a snow drift and we were pulled out by a local farmer with a front loader. He was a young man with a very kind heart and would not take any payment for it. People do really help each other around here. Even though we disagree with most people in the area politically, we find they are basically really good people. Oh, and they call a potluck a 'pitch-in' here."

I asked Cathy whether their needs for socialization are being met and if they had any challenges with making friends in their new area.

"We are still working on this. Most people here have known each other for years. Many are from old families that have stayed in the area. They are not unkind but it's kind of difficult to work your way into some organizations and you have to be somewhat determined if you want to be involved. We are active in church and the theater group. I do wish this area was a bit more intellectual and I wish we had a small college to provide some more cultural opportunities."

Overall, Cathy and Jeff are happy with their choice of where to live. Cathy occasionally posts pictures of their house with the lake in the background, and it is serene and beautiful. I asked about their long-term plans.

"We plan to remain here until we cannot anymore, physically. We remodeled our house about a year after we moved and added a master bedroom; now most of the things we need are on one level. There are a couple steps down to the laundry room and car in the attached garage. We are also considering spending time in warmer areas, perhaps Florida or Arizona, during the months of January, February, and March. But this is a few years in the future. In the next ten years we also plan on traveling as much as our bank account will allow. When the time comes, we will probably move a bit closer to the girls in the southern Indianapolis area."

I asked Cathy what advice she would offer to people who are considering retiring to a small town or rural area.

"I would say that people need to be very aware of the situation they are moving into and the distance they will have to travel for services, especially healthcare. But if the positives outweigh the negatives then it's very worth it.

"I have always wanted to live on a lake and I get to wake up every morning living that dream."

Mark and Frank were New York City residents for many years. A few years ago, when Mark was downsized from his job, they decided that it was time to move out of the city to a small house in rural western New Jersey which Frank had inherited from his grandmother.

Mark is a prolific author of murder mysteries and the editor of my first two books.

Mark explains, "We had the advantage of owning this house for a long time first. Frank has been coming here all his life. It was his grandmother's house since the 1950s. I have been coming here on weekends for the 12+ years we've been together, so I really just had to adjust to living here full time. I was ready for a life outside New York City and have had just a few adjustments, with no regrets.

"I miss having our laundry done by one of the many dry cleaners/laundry services that are ubiquitous in NYC. I didn't do laundry for 25 years, and now I do at least three loads a week at home. I also miss having a housekeeper to do the cleaning. A house is a lot more work than an apartment."

Mark took a job at a grocery store in New Hope, Pennsylvania, partly for the extra income but mainly for the health benefits.

"We have two cars now. We didn't really need a car in the city but Frank always had one. We soon discovered that you cannot successfully live in a very rural area without a second car. I use it to drive to work across the river in New Hope."

Since Mark and Frank spent weekends at this house for many years, they mostly knew what to expect. Still, I asked if anything has turned out differently than they expected.

Mark replied, "Rodents, bats, insects. We've had bats in the house every summer. We had the house 'bat proofed' two years ago. There are many sounds, especially in summer. Life abounds in the country, and it makes noises. Life in a rural setting is very different from life in a city, or even a town.

"There are lots and lots of deer. We have to drive with an awareness that they can bound out in front of the car at any time. Also, with many trees along the road, limbs can fall and power lines can come down, as they regularly do here.

"People think the country must be super safe and idyllic, that you never have to lock your doors. They don't watch enough ID Channel. Last night there was a strange pickup truck parked down the road and a state trooper showed up asking questions about it.

"I love having a huge vegetable garden. Unlike living in a town of any size, we are in the woods on 26 acres of forested land."

I asked Mark and Frank how their needs for socialization are being met.

Frank replied, "I don't know how I ever had time for a full-time job. I simply don't have enough time to do all the things I want to do out here. Since I walk every day for at least an hour I've met most of my neighbors and become very friendly with a few of them. I've also joined the local historical society, where I am a docent, and the hiking club. So, I am meeting plenty of people and I have plenty of activities."

Frank and Mark are the youngest and the only gay couple in their local senior citizens group, but they have felt accepted.

Mark relies upon his job at the grocery store for much of his socialization. "I can't say how this would change if I stopped working. Without my job I would have to volunteer or find other ways to get out of the house."

I asked Frank and Mark if they plan to live in this house for the rest of their lives. While they are enjoying living in rural New Jersey now, they realize that they will probably need to move at some point.

Frank says, "We've talked about Delaware where the taxes are super reasonable and we have friends there. I'm also thinking about a 55+ retirement community where you don't have to worry about the maintenance of the grounds and there could be a clubhouse and pool and other amenities."

Mark adds, "I love living here, but I would prefer a move to, say, Lambertville, a town I adore and where most of my fictional characters have mysteriously moved! Living in town would be great. I don't like having to drive everywhere. We live six miles from the nearest town. I cannot walk into town and that is the one thing I've told Frank I want wherever we move in the future. I want to be able to walk to a diner or cafe and enjoy breakfast. When you live in the country or most places outside a city or town, you drive. I personally do not think truly elderly people should drive and I will not do so for the safety of others when I reach a certain age.

"This is also not easy in Delaware or many places people live. We do like Delaware, but I've gotten very used to this area now that we've been here full time for over a year and a half. Eventually we will consider moving to a place that is easier for old people to live, although there are plenty of old people here! Our neighbor across the road just turned 91."

Mark offers this advice for anyone who is thinking about retiring to a rural setting.

"I suggest spending as much time as possible in the setting you're considering moving to. Isolation was a big concern when we first moved here, but a second car made a big difference, as well as a job for me. Frank being as involved and neighbor-friendly as he is made a difference for him.

"Life in a rural setting is very different from life in a city, or even a town. If you're not someone who can either keep yourself busy or someone who, like me, can spend hours a day writing or being creative, then think carefully about it."

If you are considering retiring to a small town or rural area (or if you live in one now), you should assess the distance you will have to travel to receive medical services and the quality of the care that is available within a reasonable drive. This will become more important the older you get.

———

You can learn more about Mark McNease's published books, podcasts, and other writing by visiting MarkMcNease.com.

Chapter 19

Living in an RV

In 2015, Paula purchased a motorhome with the intention of having a self-contained RV capable of visiting the United States' national and state parks as well as the cities and towns she wanted to visit.

At the time, she had just returned from spending over three years in Afghanistan and felt a desire to write and publish a book, then embark on a book tour traveling to different areas of the country. "I found that my grief from the war zone kept me from concentrating, so I decided to travel the US visiting friends, family, and battle buddies.

"One of the thoughts, in the back of my mind, about traveling and seeing the sights of the United States was that the fallen soldiers, sailors, airmen, and contractors I served with in Afghanistan could never see this beautiful land that I had served and protected over a 45-year period. Now it was my turn to see it for them and for myself. For those who are homebound I would take photos to post on social media as well as produce travel books to allow them to see these sights through my eyes, or more accurately camera lens, with a story maybe."

For Paula, the choice was easy to travel in a RV rather than to find motels along the way. "With an RV, I have the ability to camp in remote areas and enjoy nature. I can stop virtually anywhere and be spontaneous as to my time and location."

After a few months of traveling in the motorhome, Paula purchased a Jeep to tow. That opened up many more opportunities for adventure, especially exploring terrain than an RV would never be able to navigate. Next, she bought a bicycle, and then a kayak.

Many people who travel in an RV for extended periods of time tow a small car or attach motorcycles or bicycles to their RV. Having supplemental transportation means you don't have to have to leave your camp site or trailer park space unattended whenever you go out to eat, shop, or visit a local attraction. And it's much easier to park a car than an RV. On the other hand, this increases costs and decreases mileage.

Although Paula travels alone, she rarely gets bored.

"Every day is a new adventure. I enjoy meeting people. This way of life allows me to interact with many different people and only rarely see the same person twice. We stay in contact with social media and follow each other's adventures. With planning we can meet up again, but there are so many more people out there to meet and greet.

"I like that I can be alone or in a group while traveling. In a group we can do group things like sightseeing, barhopping, game playing, hiking, biking, kayaking, or sitting around a campfire. Alone I can read, write, meditate, and enjoy solitude."

Paula has been accustomed to living on her own for years. "But there are periods in which I would love to share the adventure with someone else. I work through these times by reading, writing, or finding something to occupy my hands and mind. I love to cook and plan the menu so that helps me when I'm stationary somewhere and looking for something to do."

When Paula embarked upon her journey, she hoped that some of her friends and family members would want to join her for parts of it. She discovered that her family either doesn't want to travel or they were unable to allocate enough time for a long trip because they work or go to school.

Paula doesn't plan her itinerary very far in advance, although some full-time RVers do. She is always open to spontaneity.

"I'm not sure what the primary influence is for choosing my destination. Part of the decision is based on the weather. I head south in the winter and north in the summer. I've crisscrossed the US a few times to visit friends and family but I follow the 'shiny objects' philosophy. If I see something that catches my eye, I stop and explore. It may be the world's largest groundhog, the world's largest truck stop, prehistoric archaeological digs, or a chance to pet baby alligators."

How long does she stay in any one place? "As long as it takes. Visiting the Grand Canyon was a three-day adventure. Route 66 took me a couple of months as there are so many shiny objects along the route. I spent a week in Bend, Oregon while I explored the town, kayaked the river, visited with family, and explored local museums.

"I like that I can stay as long as I want in a particular area to relax, be a tourist, or visit with family or friends. If I find myself somewhere not to my liking, I can move on."

Paula owns a condominium in Indianapolis, which serves as a home base. "I have only lived there for several months since 2007. For the most part it has remained empty. I renovated it in 2013 in anticipation of living there but I was asked to return to Afghanistan with the State Department and did."

She occasionally thinks about returning to her condo, but as long as she can still travel to adventurous places, she will continue to enjoy life on the road. "When the day comes that my health prevents me from traveling, I can return to my condo. I don't want to waste any time just sitting around waiting for life to happen, I want to make life happen for me now."

In the meantime, she has friends who check on the condo and a neighbor who collects her mail. Most of it is junk mail that can be discarded, but the neighbor will take photos of the significant items and send them to Paula by text. Most bills can be paid automatically or online.

People have roamed the country in RVs for decades. These days, thanks to the Internet, it's easier than ever to find attractions and campgrounds or RV parks, stay in touch with people, take care of personal business, and keep yourself entertained.

Advances in technology such as LED lighting, solar panels and inverters, on-demand water heaters, automatic levelers, induction stoves, and convection ovens make RV living much easier.

As with most things in life, traveling full-time in an RV has presented Paula with a couple unforeseen challenges.

"Almost two years into this adventure I was diagnosed with a rare and incurable respiratory disorder that probably came from my extended time in Afghanistan. After months of treatment I was further diagnosed with three other conditions. The challenge for me was that I wanted to continue traveling while I was healthy enough to do so but I also wanted to get the best medical treatment possible. For two years, I have returned to the Mayo Clinic in Jacksonville, FL for treatments and evaluations.

"Why would I continue traveling in the RV with this health limitation? My answer is simply, why not? I can sit in my condo and exist within four walls and occasionally venture out, or I can continue to enjoy the sights and adventures and share them with others in books or social media postings."

As a retired military officer, Paula has Tricare for health insurance which has nationwide coverage. For retirees over 65, Medicare is available nationwide.

For everyone else, most traditional health insurance plans are not a good option for full-time RVers, because the provider networks are all located in your home area. Fortunately, a few options with national coverage exist, including fixed benefit plans, short-term medical insurance (which can provide coverage for up to 364 days), and healthcare sharing ministries. To learn more about these options, visit RetireFabulously.com/quest-resources.

You can use a national chain such as Walgreen or CVS for your prescriptions since they have a national database to access your prescription records.

I asked Paula what tips she would like to offer for anyone who is considering living in an RV full-time. First and foremost, she recommends renting an RV for a short vacation to see if that is to your liking.

"There is a huge markup on new models and they only come with a year or two of warranty, except the drive train, engine, and chassis that is warranted by the manufacturer. Most folks only keep an RV for five years, so you should be able to find a decent used RV that still has plenty of use remaining.

"Buying a used RV is a real challenge the first time but it can be financially rewarding. You should get a professional appraisal or have someone really experienced go with you to examine the unit. Build a checklist of features you want that you can refer to when you're looking at a used model.

"For prices, do your research, using the Kelley Blue Book or other listings that you can find online. If a new unit lists for $120,000 then a good starting point in the negotiations is $90,000. Be willing to use their financing as they get an incentive from the financing company. If you use their lender, be prepared to put 10-15 percent down."

A good place and time to buy RVs are at large RV shows at the first of the year. The show models, which have been traipsed through by attendees, can be bought at a heavily discounted price. Also, the new model year starts in the spring, so prices tend to be discounted in January and February.

Not all RVs are well-suited for full-time living. Some RVs have mini-refrigerators, smaller stoves, smaller and less comfortable beds, more compact bathrooms, less storage space, and less insulation. These vehicles are fine for short vacations, but you will find it harder to tolerate the inconveniences when you live in the unit full-time. Larger units have full-sized refrigerators, a queen-size bed, more storage, larger batteries and water storage tank, etc., which you will appreciate having, but larger units can be harder to drive.

Most people choose full-time RV living for the adventure and for the rewards of discovering more of the country on an up-close and personal basis.

For some, however, RV living may be dictated by economic necessity. Some people with meager retirement savings must use their RVs (which are more likely to be smaller and pulled by a pickup or strong SUV) as portable homes as they traverse the country in search of temporary employment. This may take the form of seasonal employment such as retail during the holidays, working in parks or at campgrounds during high season, pumpkin and Christmas tree lots, and so forth. Many state and national parks offer seasonal employment. The pay is modest, but the deal comes with a free place to park your RV.

Estimating and Controlling Costs

Most costs associated with full-time RV living vary widely. Costs depend on many factors, such as how many miles you drive, the gas mileage your vehicle gets, the places you choose to stay, your eating habits, and more.

Some articles claim that the average RV owner puts about 5,000 miles a year on their vehicle. That seems low, but in many cases, they are towing a car and use the car for most of their day-to-day driving.

Based on blogs I have read, many full-time RVers are not as mobile as Paula. Many stay in an area for a month or more before moving on.

The most common range for expenses is between $2,000 and $2,500 a month. This doesn't include the cost of the RV, but includes everything else: gas, campground fees, vehicle insurance, health insurance, food, maintenance, entertainment, and other miscellaneous expenses.

This may sound like a lot, but if you are going to live in your RV full-time and sell your house, this is probably cheaper.

If you no longer have a physical home base, you are free to establish any state you wish as your state of domicile. This could have significant implications for saving taxes. If you choose a state with no income tax, you'll save. A state's property tax rate becomes irrelevant, because you won't be paying it. Sales tax will vary depending on where you are.

Texas, South Dakota, and Florida are frequently chosen by full-time RVers as their domicile. All three have no state income tax and they have low vehicle registration taxes. It's no coincidence that some of the largest mail forwarding services are located in Florida and South Dakota. If you use an address in one of those states to receive your mail, the government could easily consider that to be your state of domicile.

Your state of domicile will determine which healthcare plans are available to you. Florida is home to Florida Blue, one of the few plans that offers nationwide coverage.

Gas

When you live in an RV, one of the most significant costs is fuel. RVs aren't known for good gas mileage, especially if you tow a car. Mileage ranges from 8 to 23 miles per gallon, depending on the size of your unit, how fast you drive, whether you are traveling on mountainous roads, and whether your vehicle is well maintained with properly inflated tires.

Many full-time RVers control their gas costs by thinking strategically about where they will travel in the foreseeable future. Rather than zig-zagging across the country a lot, they spend more time in a region before they move on to the next.

A fifth-wheel, which is a camper pulled by a heavy-duty pickup truck with the hitch mounted in the middle of the pickup truck bed, may be your best option. They offer better mileage, and you can unhitch the trailer at your campsite and drive the truck around, eliminating the need to tow a car. The main disadvantage is that passengers must remain seated in the truck cabin while traveling, whereas people have more freedom of movement in a motorhome. Passengers can use the restroom in a motorhome without having to stop.

Campgrounds and RV parks

Most RV parks and campgrounds provide electricity, water, and sewer hook-ups. They may offer amenities such as a swimming pool or a clubhouse. But staying in RV parks and campgrounds can get expensive quickly. You may be able to rent a space for a month and save up to 50 percent, but that assumes that you will find enough things to see and do in the area to last a month.

According to WandrlyMagazine.com, the overall nationwide average cost for one night at a campground or RV park is $29.12. The actual cost varies widely across the country and based on the level of amenities the facility provides. The average for private RV parks is $38.50 vs. $22.15 for a public park (federal, state, or local). You will usually find better amenities at the private parks, but they are only worth paying for if they are amenities you will use.

Rates also vary at different times of the year. RV parks and campgrounds usually have peak-season and off-season rates. There may also be surcharges for additional vehicles, additional people, or pets. At some parks, electricity is included. At others, you are charged based on how much you use.

Costs vary widely around the country. Generally, the Southwest is the cheapest, followed by the Northwest, the Midwest, the Rocky Mountain states, the Southeast (from Texas to Maryland), with the mid-Atlantic and New England being the most expensive region.

On a state-by-state basis, Florida is the most expensive state for camping, averaging $50 per night. Florida is probably the state where demand most exceeds supply, both in the winter when snowbirds flock to the state and in the summer when families are taking their vacations.

While you're on the road, some Walmarts allow RVs to park in their parking lots for one night. You may be able to stay at a roadside rest or truck stop, although those places often impose limits on how long you can stay. However, you won't have hookups – you'll have to rely on your on-board water supply and battery, a practice called 'boondocking.'

Free or low-cost RV camping also is allowed on some public lands, mostly in the western US.

There are many other factors that contribute to how much it will cost you to spend your time on the road in an RV, for example, how often you eat in restaurants as opposed to fixing your own meals.

It's a great idea to rent on RV and take a couple trips before you buy. It's rather expensive, especially when you add the rental cost to all of the other costs described above, but money spent on a test run is well worth it. It sure beats spending a small fortune on an RV only to discover that this lifestyle is not for you.

When you live on the road full-time, you need to make arrangements for mail forwarding. There are several good mail forwarding services that will receive your mail, hold it, then forward it in a priority mail box or envelope to an address you specify. It is important that you remain at this address long enough for mail to arrive. Some offer the service of scanning your mail so you can see what you have received and view it electronically.

Like Paula, you can get a friend or family member to perform this service, but they will need to be extremely reliable and be willing to assume this task on an extended basis.

If you are thinking about living full-time in an RV, here are several topics you should consider.

- If you are partnered, will you and your partner get along well in close quarters? Will you agree on where to go and what activities to engage in?
- If you are single, will you get lonely?
- Will you miss seeing your friends and all the groups and places that are part of your regular routine?
- Are you adaptable? Can you handle minor annoyances and changes in plans? All sorts of unpredictable things can happen when you're out on the road full-time.
- Will it bother you to see doctors you don't know?
- If you are keeping your home, do you have reliable, trustworthy people who will look after it?

If you are considering buying an RV and spending large amounts of time in it, there is a wealth of advice, information, and resources on the Internet. I have included links to several good websites on RetireFabulously.com/quest-resources.

—

Paula Coffer has published two photo books chronicling her travels, *Vanishing Historic Route 66* and *Travels with Ralf*, as well as an autobiography and three books recounting her service in Afghanistan. You can find these books on Amazon and follow her adventures on her travel blog at PaulaCoffer.com.

Chapter 20

Living on a Houseboat

When you think of living on a houseboat, the first image that probably comes to mind is Tom Hanks' character in the movie *Sleepless in Seattle*, who lived in a houseboat on Seattle's Union Lake.

And then there's Otis Redding, who was living in a houseboat in Sausalito, California at the time he wrote his hit song *Sittin' on the Dock of the Bay*.

Living in a houseboat, or "floating home" as they are sometimes called, is an option most people don't even think of. Nor is it an appealing option for everyone.

There are several advantages to living in a houseboat. They can be very inexpensive to buy and ongoing costs are quite low. And of course, there's no yard work.

Some houseboats are simply small houses built on barges. They are rectangular, one or two stories, and usually have an outdoor deck. These homes are designed primarily to stay in the same place or be moved only occasionally. Some have motors and some do not. While they vary in size, a typical footprint is around 40 feet by 15 feet. That's 600 square feet of living space on the first floor, more if there's a second floor. So, it's like living in an apartment on the water.

Others look like large boats or yachts. These have more powerful motors and are designed more for moving from place to place.

The cost of a houseboat, like a house on land, can vary widely. The level of luxury varies accordingly. Prices for most houseboats can range from $20,000 for a boat that is similar to a mobile home to $250,000 for a larger, fancier, more modern boat. As with land houses, the sky's the limit. You can buy a new luxury mansion for $500,000 or more. But you should be able to find a decent home for anywhere from $50,000 to $200,000.

One you have bought the boat, annual costs average about $6,000 a year, according to several people who have written about their houseboat lifestyle on the Internet. Here is a breakdown quoting typical costs. Like everything else, actual costs vary from place to place.

- The slip fee, which is your parking space at a marina – $250 per month
- Water and electricity – $50-$100 per month
- Sewage removal – $80 per month
- Maintenance – $1,000 per year (although it is probably higher the more you move the boat)
- Insurance – $400 per year

Water and electricity are provided by the marina via hookups similar to an RV. Some owners have equipped their boats with solar panels and composting toilets, which reduces the monthly cost and enables them to live off the grid. This provides even more flexibility for moving about and places to live.

There are houseboat marinas up and down the coasts, around the Great Lakes, up and down the Mississippi River and its major tributaries, and in such European locations as London, Amsterdam, and some French canals, to name just a few.

Some of the more well-known houseboat communities, in addition to the two mentioned above, are Taggs Island in London; the Ijburg District in Amsterdam and along Amsterdam's famous canals; Scarborough Bluffs in Ontario, Canada; Tomahawk Island in Portland, Oregon; Lake Travis and Lake Austin in Austin, Texas; San Diego, California; and Ladner, British Columbia.

As with the RV lifestyle or moving to a new country, you should try it out by renting before you go all in.

Chapter 21

Living on a Cruise Ship

A lot of people, both retirees and those who are still working, enjoy vacationing on cruise ships.

Occasionally, a meme appears on Facebook or a click-bait website about a woman who eschewed living in a retirement home in favor of living permanently on a cruise ship. When asked by the unidentified author, she claimed that living on the cruise ship was cheaper than living in a nursing home. The author went on to enumerate ten benefits to retirement on a cruise ship.

Could this be Retirement Utopia for you? Just think – you could travel the world, meet new people, and never have to cook or clean!

Could living on a cruise ship really be less expensive than other options?

Memes and articles such as this should raise a red flag. As it turns out, many of the claims made in this story are inaccurate or entirely false.

However, I was surprised to learn that there really are a few people who have lived almost full-time on cruise ships for many years. I'm talking about paying customers, not the ship's crew.

Lorraine Arzt[15] traveled with Princess Cruises for over 5,000 days, cruising ten months out of every year for over 14 years, until her passing in 2014. She spent two months each year at her home in Beverly Hills visiting her family and taking care of her affairs. In the earlier years, she traveled with her husband Joe, but after he passed away in 2002, she continued on her own. She was well-liked by crew members, who took turns sitting with her after her husband died to ensure that she never grew lonely. Ms. Arzt was given the honor of christening the Royal Princess,[16] an honor usually reserved for dignitaries.

Lee Wachtstetter,[17] 86, spent nearly seven years living aboard the Crystal Serenity ship, at a cost of $164,000 a year. (Crystal Cruise Line is a high-end line that is relatively expensive.) She previously lived on a Holland America ship for three years. Ms. Wachtstetter[18] is widowed, and she stays in touch with her family using her laptop. She visits them whenever the ship docks in Miami. She sold her land-based home in order to afford her cruise ship lifestyle.

Bea Muller[19] lived permanently aboard the Queen Elizabeth II from 2000 until the ship was retired in November, 2008, at a cost of about $5,000 per month. Prior to living on the ship full-time, she and her late husband Bob took a three-and-a-half-month world cruise aboard the QEII each year for four years. After the first week on board, she was hooked. She has sailed on several different ships since then, but not continuously nor with the longevity of her residence on the QEII.

Mario Salcedo[20] has completed over 500 cruises over a period of 13 years, mostly on Royal Caribbean ships. He averages 40 cruises per year, most of which sail the Caribbean. He maintains a condo in Miami, which he visits to exchange laundry and take care of business every time the ship docks in Miami. Mr. Salcedo, who is single, isn't retired yet; he runs a portfolio management business that he can tend to while he's ashore during the ship's turnaround days or run from the ship if needed.

---

[15] https://www.youtube.com/watch?v=Q7rCvmBs9EI
[16] https://books.google.com/books?id=4jADAAAAMBAJ&pg=PA36
[17] https://www.usatoday.com/story/travel/cruises/2015/01/19/woman-pays-164k-per-year-to-live-on-luxury-cruise-ship/22030011/
[18] https://abcnews.go.com/Travel/86-year-woman-living-aboard-luxury-cruise-ship/story?id=28351886
[19] https://www.telegraph.co.uk/travel/cruises/734774/The-real-grande-dame-of-the-seas.html
[20] https://www.beyondships.com/Cruise-articles-Super-cruiser.html

Although the Liberty of the Sea is his preferred ship, he doesn't have a permanent suite on it because he sometimes travels on other ships in the Royal Caribbean fleet.

While these die-hard full-time cruisers consistently say they love their lifestyle, clearly this mode of living is not for everyone. It presents a lot of challenges. Here are twelve reality checks to consider if you are entertaining thoughts of calling a cruise ship home during your retirement.

1. Cost comparisons between cruise ships and nursing homes are faulty

Cruise ships do not provide the level of care required for assisted living or nursing homes. You should compare the cost of living on a cruise ship to the cost of living independently, whether that's your current home, a home in 55+ active retirement community, or an apartment in a continuing care retirement community before additional expenses for assisted care or nursing care kick in.

2. You can only do this if you're healthy

Medical care on cruise ships is expensive, and is only designed to deal with minor illnesses or injuries, not on-going care. While there is a doctor on board, he or she is not there to provide continuing care. If you incur a serious illness or injury, you will be hospitalized in the next port. If you require helicopter evacuation, that's extremely expensive. If you contract a contagious illness, you'll be quarantined in your room or kicked off the ship. It may be difficult to receive refills of medications you take regularly.

3. Your health insurance may not cover cruise ship medical care

Check with your carrier, but you will probably need to purchase travel insurance.

4. You won't have any real long-term friends

You will probably meet nice people on board during every cruise, but you won't see them again after the end of that cruise. Everyone you meet will be a short-term acquaintance. The ship's staff will be nice to you, but that's what they are paid to do.

5. The costs you see on cruise ship websites are only a portion of what you actually pay

On most cruise ships, you pay extra for alcoholic beverages and sodas. Internet service, which is a lifeline for most permanent cruisers, is very expensive. Similarly, cell phone roaming charges will mount quickly. Some lower-end cruise lines may offer free self-serve washers and dryers, but most cruise ships charge steep prices for laundry service.

Guided tours at your ports of call are expensive. While you probably won't avail yourself of those after your first couple visits to a port, you will often pay for taxi or public transit services if you get off the ship.

Keep in mind that quoted prices are per person for double occupancy; if you're single, there's a hefty surcharge. None of the super-cruisers above mentioned that they got a special deal from the cruise line for their continuous patronage. There are senior discounts available on some cruises, but they are usually offered only when the cruise is likely to be undersold. Since the majority of cruise customers are seniors, it's not advantageous for the cruise lines to offer senior discounts unless they need to.

6. Cruise ship rooms are small

Standard rooms are usually about 170 square feet. Bathrooms are compact, and storage space is limited. You will be able to take very few personal possessions and a limited assortment of clothes with you. If you're going to live on a cruise ship, you may prefer a larger room with a balcony, but of course those cost more.

7. You'll need to plan for interruptions in service

All ships occasionally go into dry dock for maintenance. Your ship may also book charters, in which the entire ship is leased for a private tour. During these charter sailings, you'll need to find somewhere else to stay. If the charter does not begin and end in the same port, you'll need to travel to another city to rejoin your ship – or switch to a different ship.

8. After the first few times you visit a port, it may lose its appeal

Lee Wachtstetter, mentioned above, rarely bothers going ashore because she's most likely already been to any given port several times. She enjoys the quiet times on the ship when everybody else goes ashore.

9. If you stay on the same ship, you will probably travel in the same part of the world

Ships occasionally move to different parts of the world (usually as the seasons change), but they spend a lot of time repeating the same itineraries with only minor variations. Some cruise lines do offer world cruises that take three to six months. These cruises allow you to form somewhat longer relationships with people you meet – or you could be stuck with the same annoying people for longer.

10. Most cruise ships have dress codes

Most ships have formal dinners on some nights, and they expect passengers to wear upscale casual attire at dinner and during the evenings on the other nights. This may or may not fit your style. Personally, I'm not a fan of dressing up – and certainly not every day. Some of the lower-end cruise lines have relaxed their dress codes or eliminated formal nights altogether.

11. You'll probably gain weight

Cruise ship food is delicious, but it's not diet food. It's readily available and plentiful throughout the ship. Once the novelty of cruising has worn off and you settle into a daily routine, you may be willing to forgo the filet mignon in favor of a salad and skip dessert. But that takes will power, and studies have shown that if there is food right in front of us, we'll eat it whether we're hungry or not.

12. You'll probably get tired of the entertainment

Cruise ship entertainers are talented, but how many times will you want to watch the same Broadway show tune revues? How many times will you want to hear the same comedian's jokes or listen to the same piano bar crooner? How much time and money do you want to spend in the casino or at bingo?

After processing all these considerations, if you're serious about the concept of full-time cruising, the good news is that it's easy to try it out before you fully commit.

Mario Salcedo had never been on a cruise, so when he left his corporate job and considered full-time cruising, he started by booking six cruises, back-to-back, on six different ships belonging to six different cruise lines. After that, he tried out almost every other cruise line and experienced a variety of destinations around the world for three years before settling on the Royal Caribbean line and focusing his travels on Caribbean cruises that start and end in Miami.

Chapter 22

World-Wide Nomadic Living

A former work colleague surprised many of his friends when he announced that he and his partner were getting rid of many of their possessions and they would soon be taking off for Spain. They had found a place to housesit in Cordova.

Occasionally, they would post pictures from other locations throughout southern Europe where they were staying for a few days or a few weeks at a time.

Then came Australia. They spent a lot of time exploring Australia and New Zealand. Then there were more trips to Europe and more trips to Australia. These migrations were planned not only to take advantage of seasons, but also because most non-Schengen-area citizens can only enjoy visa-free travel in the Schengen Area for a total of 90 days out of each 180 days. The Schengen Area is a network of nations in Europe that allows border-free travel within those nations for any length of time, for citizens of those nations.

Similarly, one can visit Australia and New Zealand for a maximum of 90 days at a time, but it is possible to reset the clock by exiting the country and returning (known as a "visa run").

They kept up this routine for several years, with occasional visits back to the US. While they were enjoying the adventure of world travel, they were also scouting locations where they might settle permanently.

They narrowed their choices down to four finalists: Crete; La Palma, Spain (the westernmost of the Canary Islands); Lucca, Italy; and Margaret River, a coastal town in southwestern Australia. They selected Margaret River.

Even if you are not considering relocating to another country, the idea of extended world travel might appeal to you. It certainly appeals to me!

These days, it's easier than ever to do this, thanks to websites such as Airbnb and VRBO that advertise temporary rentals and other websites that match housesitters with homeowners who will be away for an extended period of time. Links to many of these websites are listed on RetireFabulously.com/quest-resources.

When you stay in an apartment or home, not only are you saving money compared to staying in a hotel, you are also able to experience living in that area much more as the locals do. You'll be shopping in the local stores and discovering parts of the town or countryside that are outside the tourist zones.

The cost of this worldwide nomadic lifestyle varies widely, depending on the cost of your rental, how often you eat out as opposed to fixing meals at home, and what you do for entertainment. In most areas, you won't need to rent a car, but sometimes you might. And of course, costs vary widely from country to country and even within the same country. When you move from one part of the world to another, which you will typically have to do at least every 90 days, there's the cost of airplane flights.

If you sell your current home, get rid of many of your remaining possessions, and put the rest in storage, you will eliminate most of your day-to-day living expenses. This will free up money that could probably support a world-wide nomadic lifestyle.

Before embarking on this adventure, you should ask yourself the same questions that are presented at the end of the chapter on Living in an RV.

You will also need to have a good international health insurance policy. There are several companies who offer this product on the Resources webpage.

PART SEVEN

Retiring Overseas

Chapter 23

Why Retire Overseas?

If you have traveled internationally, you have probably visited charming, beautiful places and thought about how great it would be to retire there.

Sometimes this is just a temporary fantasy that fades a few days after you return home. But sometimes, weeks later, you still find yourself wondering whether the grass just might be greener on the other side of the border – or the ocean, as the case may be. And in some cases, it is.

There are many reasons why you might want to retire to another country.

You may be motivated to stretch your retirement dollars in a place with a lower cost of living and cheaper healthcare.

Maybe you want to enjoy your leisure years in a locale with a warmer climate and breathtaking natural beauty.

Perhaps you are ready for a new adventure and the opportunity to discover new lands and experience new cultures.

Or maybe you don't like the political or social environment in your country and you don't see that changing any time soon. You are willing to move so that you can enjoy your retirement in a kinder, gentler place with a government that's more to your liking.

Any of these are good reasons, but retiring overseas is a significant life change. Virtually every aspect of your current life will be impacted and disrupted. The type of dwelling you end up in will probably be smaller and simpler than where you live now. You will be leaving all of your friends behind and you'll have to make new friends in your new locale. You probably won't move most of your possessions. Depending on location, you may find some international chain stores and restaurants you recognize, but most of your shopping and dining experiences will be different. The TV shows, movies, music, sports, books, and many other recreational resources that you are accustomed to may not be available to you anymore.

If the only reason you are considering moving overseas is to save money – don't. You'll be miserable. If you can honestly say that you want to enjoy a lower cost of living *and* enjoy discovering a new country and its culture, fine. If you genuinely like the new place you have chosen to move to and it happens to be cheaper, great. But if your only motivation is to save money and you move to a cheaper place that you hate, you will resent all the sacrifices you had to make to move there and you won't enjoy your retirement.

This is obviously a major move and it's not a decision you should make without a lot of fact-finding and soul-searching. Read everything you can find about the culture of the country you are considering and its history. Learn as much as you can about its political system, its economy, and the problems the country faces.

You should visit any place you are considering moving to for an extended period of time and try to experience the area as a resident rather than a tourist before you move. And definitely rent before you buy. Buying property might not be a viable or desirable option at all.

Some people who live internationally spend just a year or two in a given place then move on to another country, rather than settling in one place permanently. They rent furnished apartments and retain very few personal possessions.

I'm not trying to dissuade you from moving to another country when you retire. It may be the best move you ever make. My intention with the section of the book is to make sure you have as much information as possible so that you can make the best decision and avoid making what could be a very costly mistake.

Most expats who have written articles about their experience or contributed to expat forums are enjoying their life in their new country and are glad they made the move.

Chapter 24

Can You Really Save Money by Retiring Overseas? Should You?

If you are facing the prospect of a retirement with the defining characteristic of financial struggle, or you are concerned that you haven't saved enough for retirement, retiring to a country with a lower cost of living might seem appealing.

The Internet is awash with stories and articles about how you can live comfortably overseas for just $1,500-2,000 a month – which is within range of most couples' Social Security checks.

These figures typically include rent for a two-bedroom furnished apartment, meals (including some meals eaten out), utilities, and Internet service. The people who write these articles claim you don't have to pinch pennies to achieve these results, nor do you have to live in squalor.

Can this be true? Such claims should reasonably raise a red flag and prompt you to think, "If it seems too good to be true, it probably is."

The short answer to this question is yes – you can find some acceptable places to live for less than $2,000 a month. The major caveat comes with how you define 'acceptable.' You will need to make a lot of lifestyle adjustments to be able to pull this off.

Even in small countries such as Panama and Uruguay, there is a wide range of housing options available. Some are modest and some are luxurious, and price tags vary accordingly. There are some very desirable areas and some not-so-desirable areas. Generally, you get what you pay for.

In order to answer this question, you need to do an honest self-assessment. Ask yourself (and your spouse, if you have one) questions such as these:

1. How adaptable are you to change?

Day-to-day life is different in other places. The pace is often slower, and service can be more leisurely. In the US, when you are expecting a delivery or repair person, you are usually given a two- to four-hour window. In many parts of the world, you'll probably be given a two- to four-day window.

In other countries, many people don't own a car and rely upon public transportation, walk, or ride bicycles or scooters.

Dwellings are smaller and simpler, and most people own significantly fewer possessions.

It makes sense that if you don't own a car, you live in a smaller home, and you own less stuff, it will cost you less to live. You will be spending less money for a scaled-back lifestyle. Could you do the same if you stayed in the US?

Familiar US stores such as Walmart, Costco, and Home Depot are present in some other countries. Local stores are generally smaller and more specialized. You won't recognize many of the brands at first. You may be able to find some familiar brands that have been imported, but they will be more expensive because of the shipping costs and tariffs.

Local customs, political viewpoints, and religious influences may be quite different from what you are accustomed to.

2. How comfortable are you in different surroundings?

Your new environment may be noisier. One couple who lives in Ecuador reports they use a rain-noise generator at night to mask the sounds that permeate their external surroundings.

You shouldn't expect other countries to be America Lite at a fraction of the price. If you expect to confine yourself to an expat community, speak English, and try to recreate the type of home and lifestyle you enjoy now, then not only will you be less likely to achieve cost savings, but you'll be shutting yourself off to all the good things a different place has to offer.

In many other parts of the world, the difference in wealth and lifestyles between the 'haves' and the 'have-nots' is even more pronounced than in the US and other First World nations. Even living on $1,500-2,000 a month, you will be among the upper class. There are slums and people living in extreme poverty in many places in these countries with a cheap cost of living. Even those who earn middle-class incomes live in homes that are noticeably more modest than you are accustomed to. It's a different standard.

Even though you won't have to live in these areas, it will be difficult to avoid seeing them or passing through them as you live your day-to-day life. How will you feel about seeing this?

3. Do you really want to do this?

If you thrive on adventure and discovering new places, you will probably enjoy this experience.

The more flexible you are and the less you come in with expectations and pre-conceived notions, the more you are likely to enjoy your new home.

On the other hand, if you are considering retiring overseas primarily as a way to save money, it's more likely that you'll be miserable.

The place you move to should truly excite you, even after several visits. It should feel right. Don't move somewhere that you think you will be able to merely tolerate.

4. How good are you at making friends with new people?

When you move overseas, you'll be leaving your friends and family behind – far behind. While the Internet makes keeping in touch easier than ever, you can't rely on these tools exclusively for your socialization. Seeing and talking to someone on Skype or Facetime is not quite the same as being in the same room with them.

People who enjoy the best experience abroad do so by making friends with the locals as well as their fellow expats. To do that, you need to learn the local language and customs. Are you willing to strike up conversations with people you encounter in your day-to-day life, or are you more inclined to mind your own business and keep to yourself?

5. Are you willing to do a lot of research and get good advice?

The real estate market and the home renovation/contractor market, in particular, operate very differently in other countries. If you move to an area with a strong expat community, get connected with them so that they can recommend reputable people and inform you about local laws and practices. If you move to an area without an expat community, you will need to do a lot of research and learning. If you're not fluent in the local language, you will be at a particular disadvantage.

If you have visited your potential destination only during their tourist season, you should experience or at least research what it's like during their rainy season and learn how hot and cold it gets throughout the year. Also find out if the area is prone to hurricanes, earthquakes, or other undesirable weather phenomena.

Learn everything you can about the local system of government, the laws, and the country's political history. Consider current events in countries such as Venezuela, Argentina, Brazil, Nicaragua, and the Philippines, and assess whether conditions exist in your new country for political upheaval and how comfortable you would feel if your new country experiences turmoil.

Talk to locals, read local news sources, and search for expat blogs to gain insight into how foreigners and minorities are accepted by the local people outside of the tourist zones. Will your religion, race, or sexual orientation be an issue?

In some countries, especially those where people are proud of their distinct heritage and traditions, most of the locals simply do not want to see foreigners move in.

6. What elements of your current environment and lifestyle would you miss?

Write down everything you enjoy that is a part of your day-to-day life – even the most mundane things. This may include the stores you shop in, the types of food you eat, your favorite TV shows, American movies, the sports you follow, the live music and arts scene you enjoy, your favorite restaurants, and so on.

What is available at the destination you are considering? What are you willing to do without? Will local alternatives be just as enjoyable as what you're accustomed to? For example, you might discover that you enjoy watching soccer matches as much as American football, and that the local baked goods and fresh fruits and vegetables are even better than what you eat now.

7. Will you be able to achieve the low cost of living these articles claim is possible?

To a great extent, this depends on whether you are willing to live more simply and adapt to living like the locals. The more you try to maintain the lifestyle you live now, the more it will cost you – especially if you import the products you are accustomed to using or you are willing to pay higher prices for them in the local stores that import them.

It also depends on how often you plan to travel home. Mexico and countries in Central America and northern South America are only a few hours from the US, but making very many of these flights will significantly eat into your savings.

The biggest difference in the cost of living is the cost of healthcare. The United States has, by far, the most expensive healthcare in the world, and costs continue to rise well above the rate of inflation every year. You will need to buy private health insurance to cover major medical events and pay for everything else out of pocket. It's still far cheaper than the US, and in many countries, the quality of healthcare is quite good. There's more information about obtaining health insurance overseas in a subsequent chapter.

Chapter 25

Where Can You Retire?

Moving anywhere is a big decision involving a lot of factors, but the decision to move overseas adds several new dimensions. One of the most significant is immigration laws.

Unfortunately, you can't just move anywhere you want to go. Every country has immigration laws. Like the United States, they don't want to have open borders which allow people to just flow into the country without meeting certain criteria.

In many cases it is more difficult to immigrate as a retiree than it is for a younger person who has years of work life remaining. In some cases, it is impossible.

Some countries welcome retirees from abroad, but most do not. Most of these countries are located in Latin America, southern Europe, and southeast Asia. Most notably, Panama and Ecuador are very welcoming of American retirees.

Other countries don't want retirees at all, presumably due to concerns about the impact of retirees on their healthcare and social systems. In most other countries, you can apply to immigrate to the country for work, for study, or if you are married to a citizen or have immediate family members who are citizens. Those categories do not include most retirees.

> **IMPORTANT DISCLAIMER:** *The information in this book is an overview provided for your convenience. I have expended a lot of time and effort researching this information, but I cannot guarantee that it is accurate. You must verify everything with the government of the country you are interested in immigrating to. Laws can change at any time. Do not make any decisions to move to another country based solely upon the information contained in this book!*

Similarly, information you find on various websites may not be entirely accurate or up-to-date. Always verify information with each country's official immigration website.

Immigration laws vary widely from country to country, but there are some criteria that are similar for most countries.

- Every country will require you to present evidence you have sufficient means (net worth and/or income) to support yourself in their country. They want to ensure you will not require financial assistance from the government. The numbers vary widely.
- Almost all countries will require a background check or police report to prove you do not have a criminal record.
- Most countries will require you to present evidence you are in good health and do not have any serious (expensive) medical conditions.
- All countries will require you to obtain some sort of health insurance. The good news is this insurance will be considerably cheaper than what you would pay in the US. You will be able to pay for most routine medical care and prescriptions out of pocket because they are so cheap. You need the insurance to cover more serious illnesses and injuries.
- Most countries have two steps you will go through on your path to becoming a permanent resident, such as spending several years in the country on a renewable temporary visa before you are granted a permanent visa.
- Some countries require a significant investment of money in government bonds or other local investment vehicles in order to obtain a visa. Depending on your financial situation, this could eliminate countries from consideration. Other countries require

an investment in property, or at least a rental agreement with a minimum value.

- Some countries prohibit you from getting a job or earning money in their country.

For many retirees, a permanent residency visa is enough. Generally, you can live in a country for as long as you want on a permanent residency visa and it's not necessary to acquire citizenship.

But if your ultimate goal is to become a citizen of your new country, there is an additional process for that which varies widely from country to country. If you are considering becoming a citizen in another country, find out whether you can have dual citizenship. Otherwise, you will have to renounce your citizenship in your current country. For United States citizens, this is a very bad idea. If you renounce your US citizenship, you are relinquishing all Social Security and Medicare benefits, and you may be subject to a hefty expatriation tax (or "exit tax"). Plus, you can't change your mind later.

These countries currently have provisions in their immigration laws which make it possible for retirees to immigrate, providing you meet certain criteria:

- Andorra
- Argentina
- Belize
- Brazil
- Chile
- Colombia
- Costa Rica
- Croatia
- Cyprus
- Ecuador
- France
- Greece
- Indonesia
- Italy
- Malaysia
- Malta
- Mauritius

- Mexico
- New Zealand
- Nicaragua
- Panama
- Peru
- The Philippines
- Portugal
- South Africa
- Spain
- Sri Lanka
- Thailand
- Uruguay

There are a few others. I haven't investigated most countries in Africa, central Asia, or islands in the Caribbean or South Pacific. That's because most of these places aren't popular retirement destinations, usually for good reasons.

Just because the countries listed above have a pathway for retired people to immigrate there, doesn't mean that they are desirable places to live. This is highly subjective. We each have our own definition of Retirement Utopia.

It's also important to remember that no country is homogenous. Even relatively small countries like Panama and Uruguay aren't the same throughout the country. Saying, "I want to retire in Panama" is just as vague and unfocused as saying, "I want to retire in the United States" or even, "I want to retire in California."

In Panama, for example, Panama City is a bustling, modern city with tall buildings and businesses and neighborhoods of all types. It has good infrastructure, heavy traffic, and most other things you would expect to find in a big city. It's more expensive to live there than any anywhere else in Panama. Outside of Panama City, you have beach towns, mountain towns, and outlying islands – all different. Some are sufficiently equipped with utilities, services, stores, and restaurants, while others are not. Some are cheap places to live and some are not.

When you start to research data on other countries, it a lot like researching data on US states and cities. Some factors are uniform throughout the country, such as its immigration policy and its tax rates.

Other factors, such as cost of living and quality of the infrastructure, can vary widely.

If you look at where expat communities are located in a country now, chances are good that these locations have a good combination of cost of living, safety, infrastructure, and overall quality of life. We'll talk more about the value of expat communities and how to find them in a subsequent chapter.

Notice what countries are not on the list.

Canada

Canada has some of the most liberal immigration policies in the world, but only if you are still of working age, an asylum seeker, or married to a Canadian. Otherwise, Canada does not provide an easy way in for retirees.

If you are a US citizen and plan to live in Canada less than six months out of every year you don't need a visa, which makes a partial-year living arrangement easy. However, access to Canada's healthcare system is only available to you if you are a permanent resident. If you are planning to stay in Canada for less than six months at a time, you'll need to purchase health insurance.

Qualifying for a permanent residency visa is tricky, since Canada considers the ability to work an important factor. But if you can prove that you have sufficient funds to support yourself, you may qualify. Higher education and the ability to speak fluent French (nationwide, not just in Quebec) are pluses. If you have funds to invest in Canada, that's another plus.

The Citizenship and Immigration Canada website does not spell out specific requirements for the above categories, but they provide an online questionnaire[21] that will help you can assess whether you might qualify for a visa.

You do not need to be a resident to purchase property in Canada or to rent it out. However, property ownership isn't one of the considerations Canada will use when evaluating your visa application.

---

[21] https://www.canada.ca/en/immigration-refugees-citizenship/services/come-canada-tool.html

Australia

You may read articles online that state that you can live in Australia if you invest a certain amount of money ($500,000 or $750,000, depending on where you plan to live) in government bonds. Unfortunately, Australia terminated its Investment Retirement Visa in November, 2018.

Now, the only apparent pathway into Australia is to invest a significantly larger sum in a business or entrepreneurial endeavor that you would operate. Parents of children who are Australian citizens can still apply for a visa, and under very specific circumstances you could get in on the basis of extended family in Australia.

For most people, the door to immigration into Australia appears to be closed, unless you are married to an Australian or you are a New Zealand citizen.

Much of Europe

Retiring in Europe is a dream of many Americans. Unfortunately, the only countries that have a provision for retiree immigration are in southern Europe: Andorra, Portugal, Spain, France, Italy, Malta, Greece, Croatia, and Cyprus. Of course, you'll be close enough that you can easily travel anywhere else in Europe, and that might be good enough for you.

All other European countries have no direct path for retiree immigration. They will only issue work visas, student visas, or visas to reunite with families. If you hope to immigrate to one of these countries, your only option might be to become a citizen of one of the nations above, where you can first reside on a temporary and then permanent residency visa, then leverage your citizenship to move to your desired country. This will take years, with the possible exception of Malta (which will be discussed later).

Caribbean islands

I have chosen not to include Caribbean islands in this book, for a variety of reasons. Some are exorbitantly expensive. For example, the Bahamas, Bermuda, and the Virgin Islands are among the most expensive places in the world. Some have high crime rates since many of the residents live in poverty. Some have poor quality healthcare. Most islands and their surrounding waters are beautiful, but there's not much to do aside from sailing and snorkeling. Most Caribbean islands are at high risk for hurricanes.

In the case of Caribbean islands where you can immigrate, many require a substantial investment in property. So, if you're seeking to retire overseas to save money, this and the overall higher cost of living probably rules out this region.

It's essential to understand the visa process and other legal requirements for becoming a resident in a foreign country. Your visa status can determine your ability to purchase property, open a bank account or qualify for a credit line, and access the country's healthcare system, among many other things.

If you decide to move forward, you can make the process easier by hiring a reputable attorney in your destination country who specializes in immigration into that country. The process is different (and often byzantine) in each country, and a reputable, experienced attorney will be able to steer you through the process much more expediently than you could on your own. The documentation you will be asked to provide is extensive, and in most cases, it must be translated into the official language of that country. Immigration attorneys have an established working relationship with the appropriate government agencies. The knowledge and expedited service you gain from using an immigration attorney will be well worth the cost.

Chapter 26

The Value of Expat Communities

When I first started writing articles about retiring overseas for RetireFabulously.com, I encouraged readers not to sequester themselves in expat communities but to focus on integrating themselves into the local community.

I still feel strongly that if you're going to move to a country where English is not an official language and is not widely spoken, you should commit to learning that country's most-spoken language. I still believe that you should not expect the country you choose to be America Lite.

But now I have a deeper appreciation for the value of having a strong English-speaking expat community to connect with. This does not have to be a community where everyone is from the United States and Canada. In Europe, you'll find that the English-speaking expat communities are comprised mostly of people from the United Kingdom and Ireland. In Chile and Portugal, many expats come from South Africa.

You will be surprised at how many elements of day-to-day life are different in other parts of the world, especially when it comes to renting or buying a home, opening a bank account, arranging utilities, and engaging with local service providers. I will cover more of that in the next chapter, but for now, I'll say that trying to learn about and navigate all of these things on your own would be a very frustrating, time-consuming, error-prone, and expensive experience.

You will be far better off to rely upon the advice of expats who have gone before you. Many of them are quite willing to help others. They were probably helped by expats who came before them, and you can pay it forward by being a resource to future expats.

There's another reason: socialization. Socialization is an important part of any well-balanced retirement, both domestic and international. Loneliness is a serious problem for many retirees. Your retirement to a new country will be far more successful if you can quickly make friends in your new locale, and you can do that most easily if you connect with people who also speak English and have similar backgrounds, customs, and cultural reference points as you. In the longer term, you should be able to make some friends among the local people, but that will happen more easily after you learn their language and customs.

Keep in mind that in some countries, the locals won't be particularly happy that you are there. Consider how immigrants are treated by some people in the US. Others have no objections to the presence of expats, but feel no obligation to help expats assimilate. Their lives are perfectly fine whether you are there or not.

There are probably good reasons why expat communities have become established in certain places and not others. People who have gone before you have discovered many things that you may not even be aware that you don't know.

I strongly recommend that you place high importance on finding a good expat community to connect with, at least for your first stop overseas. Once you have become acclimated to your new country, you can consider moving someplace else later. The Resources webpage lists several websites that have expat groups, expat forums, and a wealth of articles often written by expats.

Where are the expats now?

The United States does not officially track how many people are living in various places overseas, so any figures you find on the Internet are estimates. These figures usually include all expats including workers and students, not just retirees. Still, this information gives you some indication of where you will find good expat communities and where many people before you have chosen to migrate.

The best source I have discovered for international migration data is MigrationPolicy.org. They have an interactive map[22] that lets you discover how many people have moved between any two countries. This data covers all immigrants, not just retirees. And that's okay – a good expat network will include both employed working-age people and retirees.

Here are the non-English-speaking countries that are currently hosting the most expats from English-speaking countries (United States, Canada, United Kingdom, Ireland, Australia, New Zealand, and South Africa):

- Mexico (917,000 total, 899,000 from US, 14,000 from Canada)
- Spain (384,000 total, 309,000 from UK, 43,000 from US, 15,000 from Ireland)
- France (294,000 total, 188,000 from UK, 55,000 from US, 26,000 from Canada)
- Italy (185,000 total, 72,000 from UK, 56,000 from US, 26,000 from Canada)
- Greece (80,000 total, 23,000 from US, 20,000 from Australia, 17,000 from UK)
- Indonesia (57,000 total, 32,000 from UK, 12,000 from US, 11,000 from Australia)
- Cyprus (53,000 total, 39,000 from UK)
- The Philippines (52,000 total, 37,000 from US)
- Chile (51,000 total, 21,000 from South Africa, 19,000 from UK)
- Portugal (47,000 total, 19,000 from UK, 11,000 from South Africa)
- Brazil (33,000 total, 22,000 from US)
- Ecuador (32,000 total, 28,000 from US)

These are the countries where you will most likely find English-speaking expat communities.

After you read enough articles and visit enough expat websites and forums, you'll see that certain cities and towns tend to pop up most frequently.

---

[22] https://www.migrationpolicy.org/programs/data-hub/charts/immigrant-and-emigrant-populations-country-origin-and-destination

In the chapters that follow, I provide an overview of some of the better countries to which you can retire. I'll list some of the more prominent expat communities in those countries. But if you have your heart set on moving to a different country, you should be able to find some way to connect with people there via web-based forums and Facebook groups.

Chapter 27

Buying or Renting a Home in Another Country

Buying or renting a home in another country will be considerably different than the process you are accustomed to in the United States, or whatever your home country is.

It's easy to get swept away by the surface appeal of a place you visit, but you would be just as foolish to make an impulsive real estate purchase in what seems to be paradise than you would be to immediately marry someone you've just met. You should approach your overseas home search the same way you should approach marriage – with a sufficiently lengthy engagement period.

Give your new location a trial run for a year. Don't sell your house and your possessions until you have experienced your prospective new home during all four seasons and you're sure you are going to like it.

One option is to rent a home in your new locale. Even if you decide that you like your new location, renting first will allow you to check out nearby cities and neighborhoods, learn local laws and practices for buying a home, become knowledgeable about fair market prices. You will have time to find a good realtor, attorney, and banker and establish relationships with them. Most important, you will learn whether or not you truly enjoy living there and wish to continue living there for the foreseeable future.

Housesitting is another option. Many homeowners around the world are looking for trustworthy people to live in their homes while they are gone for extended periods of time. In exchange for the free use of their house, you will assume responsibility for caring for their pets (if they have them) and keeping their house clean and in good repair. Another advantage to housesitting is that the home will already be completely furnished, and probably with nicer furnishings than you would find in an apartment.

Most housesitting agreements run for a few weeks or months, but usually not for a full year. But you may be able to arrange a sequence of homes to live in or alternate these with longer-term Airbnb-type rentals.

In many cases, renting permanently is preferable to buying property. You may be better off to rent the entire time you live overseas and never buy, especially if you plan to return to your home country someday. Laws for ownership of property by non-citizens vary widely by country. Some countries have limitations on how much money you can remove from the country, so when you sell your home you may have trouble transferring the proceeds out of the country.

The information I present here is generalized, because the laws and practices vary widely from country to country.

For starters, in the US it's common for a buyer to use a realtor to find properties, while the seller will list their property with a different realtor. The two realtors work together to facilitate the purchase and split the commission. In most countries, that's unheard of. The realtors have no concept of working together or sharing commissions.

Each realtor has his or her own set of properties they list. If you want to see a wider selection of available properties, you need to work with multiple realtors.

There is no Multiple Listing Service (MLS) in most countries. This means that it is very difficult to determine a fair market price for a home, because you don't have access to data from other home sales to compare it with. As a result, prices vary widely. Many times, especially when the homeowner is trying to sell the house themselves, they will greatly inflate the asking price. They may do this in order to recoup all the money they have put into the house over the years, or they may do it hoping someone who doesn't know better (i.e., a foreigner) will pay it. Sometimes, they are really not interested in selling, but they will sell if the price is high enough. When they are ready to sell, the price will come down.

Now, there is an international MLS,[23] but it's hard to know how many of the locally available properties are listed on it. Several well-known real estate companies also operate internationally.

Never attempt to negotiate a purchase or rental agreement on your own. Seek out an experienced realtor and/or an attorney who specializes in real estate to assist you. International realty companies can probably refer you to one of their agents or you can ask expats for recommendations.

In some countries, realtors and contractors are not licensed or regulated. Anyone can say he or she is a realtor or contractor.

Local laws vary widely. For example, in Mexico foreigners cannot directly buy property within 50km (31 miles) of the coast or 100km (62 miles) of a land border. Buyers must establish a bank trust and buy the property through the trust. The trust will own the property, not you.

Bank financing is another tricky obstacle. US mortgage lenders will not lend money for an overseas purchase, and working with banks in another country can be a lengthy and complicated process. Mortgage rates are usually higher in other countries, and in many cases a much higher down payment is required. You'll probably find it easiest to purchase property only if you can pay for it in full.

If you do not plan to reside in your foreign home full-time, consider how it will be kept secure and maintained in your absence. If you plan to rent it out when you're not there, that presents another layer of laws to understand and arrangements to be made. Many places do not have management companies as we know them, so you'll have to find a local person you can trust to manage your property.

Real estate taxes vary considerably from place to place, so you should find a good attorney or accountant in your new home country who understands the laws. You should gain this knowledge before you buy, not afterward.

Paying taxes and utility bills is another issue. Some less-developed places in the world, including some in Latin America, are still not set up for automatic online payments. You (or a proxy) will need to pay your bills in person. Sometimes there are kiosks for paying utility bills in shopping malls or stores, sometimes you can pay at a bank, or you may

---

[23] Realtor.com/international

have to pay in person at each utility's office. You may have to pay in cash.

Chapter 28

Accessing Healthcare

As you are well aware, healthcare in the United States is exorbitantly expensive. One of the main reasons so many people are drawn to retiring overseas is that high-quality medical care and prescription drugs in most other developed and developing nations cost a fraction of the US price.

There are many reasons why healthcare costs in the US are so bloated. First, medical care for most Americans is not government-subsidized, except for Medicare and Medicaid. Second, the US system of covering virtually all healthcare costs through insurance results in a vast additional layer of costly overhead that is the insurance industry.

In most of the rest of the world, healthcare is less expensive to begin with, since medical practices have far less overhead in areas such as billing (since there's much less insurance overhead) and malpractice insurance. In addition, the government subsidizes healthcare to a much greater extent. This means that most people pay for routine medical care and prescriptions out-of-pocket because it's so cheap. Insurance is only tapped for expensive operations and disease treatments.

Health insurance in most countries operates under the same philosophy as auto insurance or home insurance in the US. With auto insurance, you don't expect insurance to cover oil changes, new tires, batteries, or most repairs. You pay for those out-of-pocket. You only file an insurance claim when you have an accident in which the cars involved are totaled or require expensive repairs. It's the same with home insurance. You only file a claim for major damages or destruction, not for minor repairs. Yet, we expect health insurance to cover virtually all costs associated with our medical care.

The second reason is that in most other countries, healthcare is considered a right for all citizens. In the United States, it is considered a benefit of employment. More specifically, it's a benefit of employment with an employer who is large enough to be able to afford health insurance for its employees. Self-employed people, people who work for small employers, contractors, and full-time students have to fund their own insurance or go without.

When you move to another country, as a non-citizen you will be required to purchase your own health insurance (usually as a condition of receiving any kind of visa), but it's significantly cheaper than insurance in the US.

Medicare will not cover you outside of the US.

Most countries have public and private healthcare systems. Each country has its own rules. In some, you won't be able to use the public system until you have a temporary or permanent visa. In others, the public system is only available to citizens. Generally, you will experience shorter wait times and better care in private facilities, plus you are more likely to encounter English-speaking doctors. You will probably prefer to use the private system rather than the public system anyway.

While researching any country you are considering moving to, make sure you learn how the local system works. The insurance you buy may cover some of the higher costs of better coverage.

Most international plans do not embrace the concept of in-network or out-of-network providers. You can use any provider you choose. However, most private international health insurers will provide a referral list of recommended doctors, hospitals, and other medical professionals that are, presumably, the better providers. These providers also have direct-pay relationships with the insurance company, so you don't have to pay the cost yourself and then seek reimbursement. You aren't required to use them, though.

Here are several of the largest international health insurance companies:

- Aetna International
- Allianz Care
- BUPA Global
- Cigna Global
- GeoBlue

Links are provided at RetireFabulously.com/quest-resources.

Other companies offer local insurance in particular countries. The people in Mexico whose stories you will read in an upcoming chapter use MetLife and United Healthcare.

Ask expats in your destination country which company and plan they use and recommend. Use a well-established company, and make sure you thoroughly understand exactly what coverage you're getting and the geographic area the policy covers.

When choosing an insurance carrier, learn whether your coverage includes international travel or just healthcare in your new home country. If your policy only covers you in your home country, then be sure to purchase travel insurance any time you leave the country.

Early in 2019, a professional flutist from Canada traveled to the United States for a flute convention. While in the US, he suffered a heart attack and had to be hospitalized. Although he had excellent healthcare in Canada, those benefits did not cover him while he was in the US. Sadly, he had not purchased travel insurance, so he amassed medical bills totaling over $100,000, which he was responsible for paying.

Similarly, if you are a US resident, you should always purchase travel insurance. You can easily cover a minor medical incident the occurs overseas thanks to their lower costs, but you would still have to pay more money than you would like if you have a major incident.

Chapter 29

Taxation and Other Financial Concerns

You probably aren't going to move to another country for the primary reason of saving on taxes, any more than you should move solely for the purpose of spending less money. These factors can be benefits, but they shouldn't be the primary reasons you move. Plus, when you move overseas you will have additional bookkeeping and paperwork to deal with, and you will need to prepare and file taxes in both your country of citizenship and your new country.

Before you move to another country, there are many factors you should consider with regard to taxation, banking, and the movement of money. You need to learn about the tax laws in your new country. It's fine to educate yourself by reading tax information online, but before you move you should meet with a reputable tax attorney in that country. You should also engage that person when you file your taxes each year. Ask the local expat community for recommendations.

Do not ask your US-based tax adviser about foreign taxes. If you've done a lot of online research, you probably know more than they do.

Tax laws vary widely from country to country. Some are advantageous for expats, some are not.

Most of the information below applies to US citizens. If you are a resident of another country, the details will be different but you will have many of the same considerations, such as how (and if) you can receive your government benefits, taxation, banking, money transfer, and so on.

In Belize, Panama, Uruguay, and Malaysia, you will owe no tax on income that is earned outside the country, including your income from your Social Security, pension, and investments.

In other countries, you will owe taxes on any money that is brought into the country, including via electronic transfer.

If you are a US citizen, it's important to note that no matter where you live in the world, you cannot escape the long arm of the IRS. You will owe US federal income tax no matter where you live. You will almost certainly benefit from using a US tax adviser to determine the US taxes you will owe.

There is one silver lining to this taxation cloud – the Foreign Earned Income Exclusion. This exclusion only applies to income you earn by working in a foreign country, not income from your retirement investments and not as an employee of the US government. So, if you get a part-time job as a tour guide or an English tutor, for example, or if you open a bed and breakfast in your new country, that income can be excluded from your US taxes up to an amount that is adjusted annually. In 2019, that amount was $105,900.

On the other hand, your visa which enables you to live in your new country may specifically prohibit you from working while you live in that country. If you do, you'll need to apply for a work visa.

Income from Social Security, your pension, and your investments does not qualify for the Foreign Earned Income Exclusion.

Speaking of Social Security, make sure you are moving to a country where you can receive your Social Security benefits and verify how you can receive them.

The US government has an international direct deposit agreement with many other countries. In those cases, your Social Security payment can be deposited directly into your foreign bank account. You should verify whether your new country is one of them. Several Southeast Asia countries that are sometimes mentioned as retirement destinations are not on this list, such as Thailand, Vietnam, and the Philippines. In South America, Uruguay, Chile, and Ecuador are not on this list. For any of these countries, you'll need to maintain a US bank account and have your payments deposited there, then transfer your money to your bank account in your new country.

If you have your benefits deposited directly into a foreign bank account, your bank will probably convert your entire payment into the local currency. If you want to keep some of that money in dollars, you'll need to have your payment deposited into a US bank account then transfer funds as needed.

Generally, the Treasury Department cannot send Social Security payments to persons in Azerbaijan, Belarus, Cuba, Kazakhstan, Kyrgyzstan, Moldova, North Korea, Tajikistan, Turkmenistan, Ukraine, and Uzbekistan. However, you can receive all the payments that were withheld once you move to a country where the Treasury Department can send payments.

It's unlikely that you'll want to retire to one of these places, but you should still verify this information.

Your US-based bank may or may not allow you to maintain your account if you do not have a US mailing address. You might be able to use the address of a family member or a Post Office box, but you should check with your bank to be sure.

Money you move into a foreign banking system needs to be reported. US citizens or permanent residents are required to fill out a form to declare the amount of money in foreign bank accounts, brokerage accounts, mutual funds or other financial accounts if the value exceeds $10,000 at any time during the calendar year, or if the person has financial interest in more than one account.

You will probably want to maintain a US-based credit card, so select one that does not charge a fee for international transactions. Some financial institutions, such as Charles Schwab, will refund ATM fees you incur when using a foreign ATM.

This chapter is not intended to be a definitive or complete resource for taxation and movement of money internationally. It's just an overview that is intended to alert you to the multitude of matters you will need to consider. Always seek professional advice and refer to government websites for the most accurate information.

Chapter 30

Culture Shock

When you move to a new country, whether it is in Europe, Latin America, Asia, or anywhere else, you will inevitably experience culture shock. You'll experience culture shock in many ways, extending over the course of months or even years.

People who come to the United States (or whatever your home country is) experience culture shock too.

Life in other countries is different. Holidays and customs are different. The pace of life is different. Laws and societal norms are different. You will be able to fill a book with the ways that things are different. It's not necessarily better or worse, it's just different.

Maybe some characteristics of society in your home country are better than those in your new country, but it doesn't matter. You can't change things in your new country, you have to embrace them and adapt to them. If you can't (or won't), you'll have a miserable experience, and you should seriously reconsider your plan to move there.

One of the joys of traveling to other places is learning about how other people live. When you travel, you just get a glance. When you move to a new place, you are immersing yourself in it.

If you look at it the right way, culture shock is good for you. It increases your adaptability. It broadens your world view. It improves your skill at dealing with people who are different from you.

Learn as much about your new country as possible before you move there. You will probably be introduced to many aspects of the culture of your new country when you visit. Still, once you get there, you will experience culture shock.

You will probably go through several stages as you adapt to your new country. Your journey through these stages will be unique to you, and it won't conform exactly to this list. But you will go through stages, one way or another.

Typically, the stages play out something like this:

1. The honeymoon

Everything is new, wonderful, and awe-inspiring. This new adventure is exciting! There's a whole new world opening up before your eyes. It's fun to explore your new surroundings and discover where everything is. You're a tourist on an extended vacation.

2. The honeymoon is over

Everything is annoying, inferior, and smelly. Everything you do involves compromising and settling for less. Doing even simple everyday things is challenging and frustrating. Nothing is as good or works as well as back home. People aren't going out of their way to welcome you and befriend you. The people are rude and have the audacity to not even speak English!

3. Turning the corner

You decide that things aren't so bad. You become more comfortable with the language and the local practices and customs. The annoyances seem more minor and they become less frequent. Challenges seem more manageable. You can do this!

4. Acceptance

You have acclimated to your new surroundings. You've made friends, joined some groups, and discovered where the good restaurants and shops are. You've taken some side trips and discovered some beautiful places. All those little things that used to irritate you no longer do. It's just how things are. You realize that you like it here and you're glad you made the move.

There's one event that could happen at any time, especially during stages 2 and 3:

The panic attack

It hits you like a brick. You're in a strange land many miles from home. Your friends are thousands of miles away, and you have no real friends here. You're lonely. You don't fit in. Everything is different. Your internal voice is screaming, "OH MY GOD, WHAT HAVE I DONE?!?!?" This whole thing has been a terrible mistake, and you want to catch the next plane home.

Relax. Everyone experiences this, maybe several times. It will pass. Don't hunker down and hide from the world, force yourself to go back out into it. Like most other problems or changes in life, the sooner you face them and deal with them, the sooner you can move on and start enjoying life again.

The re-entry

Someday, if you move back to your home country, you may feel a sort of reverse culture shock. Things changed. Your friends' lives went on without you. People are in a hurry and they seem so stressed. Many things are more expensive. You may even miss your adopted home.

I have collected some advice from my own experience and many other sources about the various ways you might experience difference when you move to a new country. Not all of these will apply to all countries, since each country and each region are different. But many of these are fairly common experiences.

1. Differences in communication style

In some cultures, especially in Europe and the US, people communicate openly and directly. They may even seem forceful and brusque. In other cultures, communication is more subtle and nuanced. In some cultures, it takes time to build a relationship with people before you can truly enjoy open communication with them.

In Asia especially, it's all about saving face. People go to great lengths not to say or do anything that will embarrass others. That may lead to cases where information isn't shared or is only hinted at, in order not to embarrass anyone.

2. Differences in humor

What are and are not acceptable topics for humor is different everywhere. In some places, such as Ireland and some Latin American countries, teasing or poking gentle fun of people isn't intended to be offensive, it's an attempt to break down barriers. Teasing you is usually a sign that they like you, or want to like you. In any case, it's harmless.

Topics that are considered politically incorrect in the US may still be fair game in other societies, like it or not.

3. Differences in time standards

This is well-known and well-documented, both in this book and in most other books and articles about living overseas, but in most of the rest of the world people are more lax about keeping time commitments. People simply aren't punctual. People don't take life as seriously, which in many ways is a good thing. In the Unites States, life can be too fast-paced and stressful.

While the more relaxed and laid-back culture may be refreshing, it can also be very frustrating to wait several days for someone to show up to repair or deliver something, never knowing for sure when (or if) they will actually arrive.

4. Differences in living standards

One of the main reason that housing prices are so much lower in many parts of the world is that houses are much more modest. Working-class people live in smaller, simpler dwellings. While you're likely to find a nice TV inside and a satellite dish on the roof, you won't see many of the kitchen appliances and other trappings of First World middle-class living we take for granted.

Try to remember what our homes were like in the 60s and 70s, before microwave ovens, Cuisinarts, coffee-makers, stand-alone freezers, PCs and laptops, home theater systems, and multiple cars. That's how many people in the rest of the world still live. It's all they can afford. Remarkably, they aren't sad that they don't have these things – they may actually be happier.

When you compare a city in Latin America, Asia, or some cheaper countries in Europe to your home city, you'll see that many prices are cheaper there. But look at the line for purchasing power, which is a measure of how much people can afford based on their pay. The purchasing power in the location you're looking at will always be significantly lower.

The neighborhoods where the locals live might look almost slummy to us, but it's normal to them. They are probably safe. It's just a different standard.

If you live in a nicer house in an area developed especially for First World expats, this will contribute to the perception that you are rich and privileged – because you are.

It may be uncomfortable to see children selling candy on the streets instead of attending school or poor people peddling jewelry and crafts, especially when you realize that a good day or a bad day of sales makes the difference between whether or not they eat. In First World countries, you rarely come face-to-face with extreme poverty.

5. Differences in customer service

Whether you're dealing with a government agency or simply trying to get served by a waiter or store clerk, you'll find that service in most places is more casual and leisurely, if not totally disengaged.

Transactions such as opening a bank account or turning on a utility, which can usually be accomplished with a brief office visit, phone call, or even online in a First World country, could take days or even weeks in a less developed country.

You could discover that a person you had an appointment to meet with just took off on vacation for two weeks.

Again, the pace of life is slower and the standards are different.

6. Differences in attire

This will vary widely from place to place, but chances are good that the everyday people will dress differently that you are accustomed to. Pay attention to this when you go on visits. In many places, it's inappropriate to show as much bare skin as we do in the US. People in other countries may be less inclined to wear shorts, even when it's hot. You'll probably see fewer bright, bold colors and patterns.

In addition to standing out as a foreigner (which will be obvious enough anyway), in some places with more conservative conventions, you could be denied service or entry into some places if you are dressed inappropriately. For example, if you wish to visit a cathedral, they usually prohibit shorts and upper garments which do not cover your shoulders.

7. Differences in public facilities

You wouldn't think that something as basic as restroom facilities could be so different, but they are.

In some places, toilet paper may not be provided or reliably kept in stock. In some places, such as some areas of Mexico, you're not supposed to flush toilet paper. Personally, it would take me a while to get used to the idea of leaving used toilet paper in a trash receptacle.

In Asia, you're likely to find some public restrooms where they have squat toilets. Usually, they have a mix of conventional toilets (that is, conventional to westerners) and squatty potties. In cases where a restroom has only conventional toilets, sometimes people will climb up onto the toilet seat so they can squat, leaving the dirt from the bottom of their shoes on the toilet seat.

In Europe or Latin America, don't be surprised to find the restroom staffed by a poor, unfortunate soul whose livelihood is dependent upon handing you a paper towel in exchange for a tip. You will occasionally see pay toilets.

On the other extreme, in Japan even the public restrooms are usually equipped those high-tech toilets that have the little arm that comes out and sprays water you-know-where. It's a little odd at first, but I quickly came to like them. And in Japan the restrooms, like everything else, are immaculately clean. Quite the opposite is true in other parts of the world.

8. Gestures

Hand gestures mean different things in different cultures. For example, the 'okay' sign (index finger touching the thumb, forming a circle) shows approval in the United States. In Japan, it indicates money. In France, it means zero. In Brazil, it's the equivalent of flipping someone off. A thumbs-up is offensive in some cultures, too.

In some cultures, it is rude to point with one finger; point with your extended hand instead.

Shaking hands is somewhat universal, but in some cultures the customary greeting can range from a slight bow to a hug or a kiss on each cheek.

The types of physical contact that are acceptable vary widely around the world.

In the United States, the United Kingdom, and some other western cultures, maintaining eye contact conveys interest and attentiveness. In other cultures, particularly Asian and Native American cultures, it's disrespectful, uncomfortable, or even rude.

9. Reverse discrimination

In many parts of the world, particularly Latin America and southeast Asia, if you are white, you may immediately be viewed as rich and privileged – and a target. In many cases, you are richer than the locals.

Years ago, I had the opportunity to visit Malaysia on a business trip. One evening, my local hosts took me to one of their night markets. Here, vendors set up stalls selling all kinds of merchandise – shoes, clothing, purses, watches, jewelry, electronic devices, CDs and DVDs, you name it. There were many high-end name brands (Nike, Louis Vuitton, Rolex, etc.) at unbelievable low prices! Of course, they were all counterfeits and bootlegs manufactured in China or some other southeast Asian country. Despite the fact that I was accompanied by three Malaysians, I was singled out. Every vendor leapt out at me. To them, I had dollar signs tattooed on my forehead.

Many of the most highly-touted foreign retirement destinations are in Latin America. If you are from the US or Canada (or another predominately white, English-speaking country), you will be a gringo. If you're not careful, you will be charged gringo prices for houses, services, and anything else that doesn't have a price tag already on it. To be clear, most people you'll meet will be honest and they will not try to take advantage of you – but some will.

Being a gringo may make you a higher-profile target for robbery and theft.

You will constantly have to deal with the stereotype that you are a walking ATM.

If nothing else, you will always stand out in a crowd and you may often be stared at, especially in Asia.

10. Sexism

In some countries and some parts of the world, the differences in how men and women are treated are more pronounced than they are in the United States. Gender roles that have become outdated in our society are still prevalent in many places.

You will experience differences in what is and is not acceptable behavior towards women. Sad, but true.

———

Perhaps the best way to deal with all of these factors is to approach moving to another country with as few expectations and pre-conceived notions as possible. If you try to apply the societal standards that you are accustomed to in your new country, you'll experience a lot of conflict, both within yourself and with others. If you approach the move with few expectations and a sense of discovery and adventure, you will have a happier, richer experience.

There are several good articles about adjusting to different societal norms and dealing with culture shock on RetireFabulously.com/quest-resources.

Chapter 31

Resources for Planning your International Retirement

These days, it's easier than ever to research potential retirement destinations. I will list some excellent websites below, but keep in mind that websites have their limitations.

Any website that is written and maintained by individuals is likely to be based on those people's personal experiences and preferences. This disclaimer applies to this book and to RetireFabulously.com. The information on these websites is useful in many ways, but it's not guaranteed to be factually accurate. Information changes regularly, and an article that was accurate when it was written five years ago may no longer be up-to-date.

This is particularly true when it comes to recommendations for wonderful cities where you can live cheaply.

For many years, two places that have appeared in practically every article about where to retire overseas and every top ten list are Boquete, Panama and Cuenca, Ecuador. These places have been and still are very cheap and appealing places to live. But as word about these low-cost Retirement Utopias spread, more people started moving there. Boquete is still less expensive than the United States, but prices have been going up and should continue to do so. Some people who moved to Boquete ten years ago because it satisfied their budget requirements are now feeling squeezed, as are the local citizens.

Prices in Ecuador are rising, too. It should remain cheaper than the US for years to come, but the advantage will probably shrink.

For immigration laws, always use a country's official website as the authority.

Expat Guides and Forums

One of your most valuable sources of information is expat forums and Facebook groups.

Don't be bashful about asking questions and participating in discussions. The expats who participate in these forums and Facebook groups do so voluntarily because they want to help others. My only suggestion is to limit each posting to one topic, rather than posting a long list of questions all at once.

Keep in mind that expats are not necessarily retirees. People are also living in other countries to work or study, or simply because they want to. That's okay. Most of their experiences with adjusting to and living in their country will be applicable to you too.

Here are several websites with active expat forums and other valuable information. There are active links on RetireFabulously.com/quest-resources, along with more options.

ExpatExchange.com – Lots of good articles and country forums in which individual residents share their advice and experiences. While each individual's experience in a country is different, it's valuable to read insights from real people as a contrast to the rose-colored articles you see on many websites. This website contains a lot of useful information about healthcare, real estate, shipping possessions, mail forwarding, banking, etc. It has a section that is specifically focused on retirement.

Expat.com – This website has forums for practically every place on earth. It claims to have 2.5 million members in 500+ cities in 197 countries. Most content is user-supplied, and the site contains lots of articles in the Magazine section. It's not specifically focused on retirement.

Expatica.com – This website serves all expats, not just retirees. It provides expat guides for France, Spain, Portugal, South Africa, and several other countries that don't offer retirement visas, as well as a Global guide. Their information is very thorough.

TransitionsAbroad.com – This website is a little more focused on working and teaching abroad, but it has a lot of good information about living and traveling abroad. There are plenty of articles about the expat experience.

JustLanded.com – Offers thorough, comprehensive expat guides to almost 70 countries as well as expat groups, a directory of companies providing services to expats, and property information.

Internations.org – This website offers guides to 200 cities and claims to have expat groups in 420 cities. In each, there are various events and activity groups. You will need to provide an email address to access the information. They produce an annual report called Expat Insider that rates and ranks practically every country in the world based on surveys from over 20,000 expats from all over the world.

BestPlacesInTheWorldToRetire.com – Despite its name, this website contains comprehensive information only on Mexico, Belize, Nicaragua, Panama, and Portugal. It has a Worldwide section with some information of general interest, including plenty of stories from expats about their experiences.

Safety Information

Visit the US State Department's website at **Travel.State.Gov**. They have a variety of useful articles about international travel, including articles focused on specific segments of the population (LGBT, women, faith-based, etc.) and well as information about every country. While there, you can sign up for the Smart Traveler Enrollment Program (STEP) and receive occasional alerts about safety concerns for countries you are considering traveling or relocating to.

The CIA World Factbook[24] is an excellent way to learn more about a country's background, stability, and current affairs.

Crowd-sourced safety data is also available on Numbeo.com.

---

[24] https://www.cia.gov/library/publications/the-world-factbook

Chapter 32

Retiring to Mexico

Depending on which data source you read, between 900,000 and one million US citizens have expatriated to Mexico, more than any other country. The Social Security Administration sends around 440,000 payments to Mexico each month.

It's easy to understand why. The close proximity to the US allows easy travel back and forth. On average, you can live in Mexico for about half the cost of living in the US, although that varies widely depending on which area in Mexico you choose and which area of the US you are moving from. If you're seeking a warm climate, good food, varied cultural and recreational options, and inexpensive, excellent healthcare, Mexico is a great choice. It's also relatively easy to obtain a residency visa.

In the larger cities, you'll find many familiar American restaurant chains and stores such as Home Depot, Costco, and Walmart. This could be a plus or a minus depending on your point of view.

Mexico is a large country with distinct regions and varying climates, offering you numerous options for where to relocate and many places to explore once you're there. Here are some areas that are popular destinations for expats.

There are large expat communities in Chapala and Ajijic, on the shores of Lake Chapala, about a 45-minute drive south of Guadalajara,

Mexico's second largest city. An estimated 4,000 US and Canadian expats live in this area.

San Miguel de Allende, in Guanajuato, mixes history and colonial architecture with a modern cosmopolitan lifestyle. It's popular with artists and expatriates alike.

Merida, the largest city on the Yucatan Peninsula, is rapidly growing in popularity with expats. It is hot and humid year-round and gets extremely hot in the summer, but it offers a lot of culture, excellent infrastructure, and modern amenities. The Yucatan peninsula is also very safe.

If you're looking for a beach destination, Mexico has many to consider. Of course, most of these are popular tourist areas which command higher prices.

Puerto Vallarta is a lovely coastal city with a charming colonial town center and an ever-growing array of resorts and vacation homes. PV has long been popular with tourists (especially gay tourists) and with American expats. Thanks to tourism, the area enjoys a prosperous economy and, therefore, a lower crime rate. Nuevo Vallarta, just north of Puerto Vallarta, is an insulated enclave of beachfront resorts, golf courses, and nicer homes catering to northerners.

Los Cabos, on the tip of Baja California, encompasses Cabo San Lucas, San Jose del Cabo, and other nearby towns. The climate is ideal and the area features excellent beaches, golf courses, medical facilities, and restaurants. As a popular tourist destination, it is relatively expensive and sometimes crowded. La Paz and Todos Santos, just north of Los Cabos, offer a somewhat less commercialized environment.

Other beach towns to consider are San Filipe, Ensenada, and Playas de Rosarito in Baja California, and Playa del Carmel/Riviera Maya in Quintana Roo, between Cancun and Tulum.

Let's meet two couples who have retired to Mexico. Their particular circumstances are unique, but many aspects of their stories are similar to what most expats experience when they move to Mexico and most other Latin American countries, or anywhere else in the world for that matter.

Terry and Brian have been a couple for over two decades. For most of that time they have shared the dream of retiring in a tropical beach location. Over the course of many years, they traveled to a variety of locations to discover places that might satisfy their criteria for an ideal retirement destination.

Terry explains, "Because of ties with our family and friends in Ohio we thought that staying within North America would be best. We never found the Atlantic to be overwhelmingly beautiful and it is pricey and crowded. The coast of the Gulf of Mexico didn't excite us either. For us the magic just wasn't there. We love the Pacific Ocean and the western coast of North America. Southern California is very appealing but the cost of living is really expensive. Hawaii is spectacular but we don't like the travel distance to get there and back. We still want family and friends to be close enough to visit conveniently. We explored the US Virgin Islands and there was some appeal, but we weren't sure that the island life was for us. We wanted to have a way to travel by land to return to the US.

"That left Mexico. Our first visit to Cabo San Lucas, at the southern tip of the Baja California peninsula, was around 2010. From that first visit we felt there was something special and it could be the ultimate place that met our vision. It has beautiful beaches, gorgeous mountains, year-round sunny and warm climate, reasonable cost of living, great culture and restaurants, and it's not terribly difficult to overcome language issues. Being a tourist town with a lot of Americans living here full or part time, English is quite prevalent. We returned to Cabo on vacation with friends several times.

"In 2012 we decided to start house shopping. We decided that investing in a vacation home that we'd ultimately retire to would be ideal. We found a great community with fantastic ocean views at very reasonable prices. We built a brand-new home and over the next year we vacationed there quite a bit. At the time our plan was to retire within the next five years and move into our house in Cabo full-time. My aged mother lives with us and she would move to Cabo as well.

"Brian and I worked for the same company in Ohio for many, many years. In late 2013, the company downsized and Brian's position was eliminated. We considered accelerating our retirement plans, but Brian was offered a fantastic job opportunity in southeast Florida. I was able to request a nice severance package, so I left the company too. While Florida was not on our roadmap, it was a good opportunity to get into a warm climate and try a new location.

"So, in 2014 we relocated to Lake Worth, Florida. Florida was a great experience. We enjoyed the weather except for the rainy summers and the occasional hurricane, met many wonderful new friends, and gained experience and confidence in uprooting and going someplace entirely new. But we found that it was hard to find a really excellent restaurant, the landscape was not very pretty, and because the state is flat, we never saw the ocean unless we were right on the beach. The beaches were not pretty at all. Florida is also very, very crowded, especially during the winter months when the snowbirds arrive.

"Ultimately we stayed for four years. We probably would have stayed a year or two longer but we decided to make the move to our place in Cabo in 2018, when my mom was 91 years old. While she's in great shape physically and mentally for a 91-year-old, a long move like that is difficult and we felt that if we waited longer, relocating her would be very difficult or impossible. So, we sold our home in Florida and made the permanent relocation to our home in Cabo."

Because Terry and Brian made many trips to Cabo over an eight-year period, they had a good idea of what to expect when they moved there permanently. Still, the move required some adjustments and the reality of day-to-day living is different from staying there for a week or two at a time.

As Terry explains, "For the pure vacationer, the city is mostly cocooned with gorgeous resorts, beaches, marinas, golf courses, dining spots, and of course the Sea of Cortez and Pacific Ocean. As locals, we have to venture out almost daily into the 'real' parts of town which aren't anywhere as glamorous and beautiful as the tourist cocoons.

"For the most part, Mexico is still a developing country. Most of the local areas are quite harsh in appearance. An American who is used to the typical Main Street, Anytown, USA would see these parts of Cabo as almost ghettos or slums. These neighborhoods are where most of the middle-class local residents dwell. They are actually quite safe. It is simply a different standard. The locals live more humbly than what most Americans would consider acceptable.

"We visited here many, many times before moving here full time so we became accustomed to the whole town, inside the tourist areas and out. If someone only spent time here as a tourist and suddenly moved here full time without getting the full lay of the land, they might be in for quite a shock.

"The pace is very, very slow here. Businesses operate on a very different schedule. For example, opening a bank account can take a week or more, whereas you can open a new bank account on the spot in the US. I somewhat expected it from our frequent visits here and dealing with property managers remotely from the US, but living it full time is still different than what we'd known from the US. I've had to learn a great deal of patience living here, and I expect nothing to be quick and easy.

"We are taking Spanish lessons three days a week. We started here as English-only speakers which is a little challenging but not impossible. Cabo is a tourist town, so many of the locals speak English. The challenge is going into town and trying to do business with a local merchant or bank where employees speak no English. Translation apps have become our best friend, and there is usually a customer or someone nearby that will jump in and help translate if needed.

"Learning Spanish has been a lot of fun. I spent many years in my career computer programming and learning Spanish has been somewhat like learning a new programming language. When I learn new words and phrases, I'll try them out in town at a restaurant or store and see if it works, sort of like trying to test compile a computer program. Sometimes it works, sometimes it doesn't. But most of the time the locals are happy when an American is trying to learn Spanish and they like to help teach us new ways of saying things.

"We socialize with both local people and other expats. In our neighborhood, most people here are retired English-speaking Americans. We've become friends with many of them. We've also met and made friends with several Mexican natives. Very few Mexicans living in Cabo are true Cabo natives. Most have transplanted from other parts of Mexico. Most speak English although we are good friends with one guy who speaks almost no English. We communicate with him mostly in Spanish/Spanglish and using a lot of Google Translate.

"The Mexicans treat expats very nicely. They are a very good-natured and kind culture. In fact, I would say that expats are often treated nicer than we are sometimes treated in the US by our fellow citizens.

"We've had no worries about being a gay couple here in Cabo. The LGBT community is small. Cabo isn't particularly known as an overtly gay town like Puerto Vallarta, but it is gay friendly. There is only one gay club, although we've never visited it. We have met several LGBT individuals and they all seem comfortable with being open here. There is even a pride parade each year, although it is very small."

In addition to the beautiful surroundings, near-perfect weather, and lower cost of living, one of the biggest advantages to living in Mexico is their healthcare system. The quality is comparable to the US, but at a fraction of the cost. Most prescriptions and medical services are cheap enough to pay out of pocket. Health insurance is only needed to cover more expensive procedures.

"We purchased our health insurance through a global insurance company that is underwritten by United Healthcare. It runs a little less than $1000/month and typically requires upfront payment to the provider with subsequent reimbursement by the insurance company. Prescription meds here are typically very cheap. For example, the pre-insurance price in the US for a one-month supply of a medication I take was around $140. Here I can buy a one month supply the same medication for less than $5!"

I asked Terry if they had any issues with buying real estate in Mexico. They had no serious issues, but "it's important to understand that in Mexico, foreigners cannot own land outright in a 'restricted zone,' which is 100 km from a border with another country or 50 km from the coastline. So that means our house is held in a trust and we pay an annual maintenance fee on the trust. I think it is something like $900 a year.

"It is also much more difficult to get a loan to purchase a home or property in Mexico. US lenders do not lend money for the purchase of foreign property. Mexican banks will lend money but typically they require 50% down payment. Many real estate transactions are full cash deals.

"Closing costs and realtor fees are also pretty expensive. Realtor fees can run in the 8-10 percent range. Selling real estate can actually be more difficult than buying with all of the costs. Because of the difficulty of getting loans, many sellers offer some sort of financing themselves. Typically, a seller may want 30-50 percent down and take payments over a few years on the balance, charging somewhere in the 7 percent interest range."

Terry and Brian's home is a modern, upscale home in one of the tourist/resort cocoons less than a mile from the beach. They can see the ocean from their home, which was a criterion they valued highly when choosing their home site. Now that they have settled into a day-to-day routine, they don't go for walks on the beach nearly as often as they thought they would.

Homes in these expat cocoons are considerably more expensive than most other homes in Mexico, but they are comparable to the median house prices in many parts of the US. If their house was located in a similar community near the ocean in southern California, Terry pointed out, it would cost several million dollars. Property taxes for their home in Mexico are a small fraction of what they would be in southern California. So, their home in Mexico is a bargain for what they're getting.

Terry offers this advice for anyone who is considering retiring to Mexico.

"Take a lot of time, do your research, visit many places. A lot of people recommend renting a place and staying for a year before buying property which I think is sound advice. Try to learn at least a working level of the local language. Join relevant Facebook groups where others living in the same region have the same questions or advice about moving and living there. Lay out a detailed plan and include every small detail you can think of. Consider banking, how you will get money from the US to yourself, healthcare, travel, evacuation if needed, preparedness for natural disasters, ease of visitors coming in, residency requirements, and whether you will need to have a car."

Rob and Roy, a couple from Oregon, decided to leave the rat race and retire early. According to Rob, "we needed to find a place with a low cost of living. In addition, Roy wanted very much to live on the water and try his hand running a bed and breakfast. The cost of living in the US and the cost of coastal real estate in the US pushed us to look at options outside the US. While there was lake and riverfront real estate in the US we could afford, they were not ideal locations for a B&B and, again, US cost of living would have increased the risk of us running out of money.

"Both of us were married before and we have seven children between us. We wanted to make sure that we could afford to visit them or have them visit us on a routine basis, so cost of transportation was a major factor. In researching flight costs, we discovered that Cancun has some of the lowest cost flights around. It would be cheaper to fly to Cancun than almost any other location, including even budget flights to south Florida.

"However, waterfront property in Cancun is not cheap. We therefore looked at waterfront properties within a reasonable driving distance from the Cancun airport. That Internet-based search led us to properties east and west of Progreso on the Yucatan Gulf Coast."

They bought a charming property in the small town of Chelem, on the north side of the Yucatan peninsula facing the Gulf of Mexico. It's on a long, narrow stretch of land separating the gulf from inland waterways. It's just west of Progreso, a town large enough to have stores and restaurants to satisfy their day-to-day needs. The nearest large city is Merida, about 50 km inland. United, Delta, and American Airlines all serve Merida, while the Cancun International Airport is almost 4 hours away.

"From pictures on the Internet, it seemed like we could get an amazing waterfront house for around $200,000 USD. We contacted a realtor, flew down to Cancun, rented a car and drove to the area. The rest, as they say, is history.

"I should point out that it was not what we expected from the pictures. The color of the sand is not the pure white color of the Cancun beaches and the water is not the crystal-clear blue waters of Cancun either. The sand is beige and the water is emerald green. Also, most houses in the area are beach houses that are used only six weeks a year. As such, the area looks like it is filled with abandoned houses. However, we found some beautiful affordable properties, like houses of the rich and famous, that made us say it would be paradise to live in a house like this. After living here, we found that the area has a lot more to offer than we expected, so we have been very pleasantly surprised.

Like Terry and Brian, Rob and Roy found that living in Mexico requires some adjustments. With the additional considerations of renovating a house and starting a business in Mexico, they encountered a lot of differences in standards and practices.

"This is Mexico! This is not the US! Deliveries will not be on time. There isn't even postal mail delivered to our house. Work is not done on time. Walls and windows are not straight or level. Time here runs on a different schedule, and you just have to accept it. Public toilets don't have seats, and used toilet paper is not flushed. Construction is done differently. There may be no ground wires, plumbing that can't accept toilet paper, and utilities that may or may not work. You need to come here with a relaxed attitude; people with Type A personalities will go berserk. If you are laid back and look at everything with a 'does it really matter' attitude, you will have a great time.

"Items are not always available. For example, when we built our pool, we found lounge chairs that we fell in love with. Since the pool was not ready, we didn't buy them and planned to buy them when the pool was finished. Unfortunately, when we went back, they were not available, and wouldn't be available for several months. The same is true with a type of coffee we like. If we don't buy it when it's in stock at Walmart, it can be weeks or months before they have it again. We have learned to buy things we like when we see them, even if we don't need them right then.

"Renovating and building is another fun topic. Everyone seems to be a contractor. Some are good and some are not. Prices quoted may be accurate or they may not. Some may do things like you expect, like 3-prong outlets with ground wires vs. 3-prong outlets where the ground isn't connected, others won't. Here is a great anecdote. We got a quote to have a bathroom built with a window and a door. When it was finished the bathroom had an opening for the window and the door, but had neither an actual window nor a door.

"Setting up our business was another fun exposure to Mexican bureaucracy. First, we had to have a will, which has to be handwritten in a special book in Spanish! Next, we needed a tax ID number. That was all well and good except that our residency cards had pictures which the copy machine couldn't copy. It took three weeks of back and forth between the local office and Mexico City to get the copies accepted.

"Mexican paperwork is a pain in the rear. You will need a good lawyer. Mexican bureaucracy can drive you nuts. You basically need an original electric bill in your name at your address to do almost anything. Electric bills are only delivered, and our area doesn't have mail delivery. Everything is doable, it just takes time and is never as straightforward as it seems. It's no surprise that a lot of business is conducted 'under the table.'

"Then there is the tax reporting. You need a government issued invoice for everything. If you buy a screw at Home Depot, you get a receipt, then walk over to a terminal, enter the information, and get an official invoice from the government. That has to be submitted back to the government within 30 days, usually by your accountant, to claim the expense.

"Realtors are not regulated. Almost nothing is regulated, with the possible exception of environmental beach controls. The first realtor we contacted turned out to be a major thief. Talk to people and get recommendations. Join Facebook groups of people who live in the area. There are a lot of bad hombres around, but there are a lot of good ones too. It's up to you to avoid the bad guys.

"Just because a house is listed for sale, doesn't mean the owner is selling it. Just because the owner asks for a price does not mean that they won't want more before you close. That's why you need good representation to help you through the intricacies."

In spite of all the annoyances and complications, Rob and Roy enjoy living in Mexico, and it meets their expectations for a lower cost of living.

"The things we like most are the ability to live right on the water, the expat community, the convenience of grocery shopping and all other necessities, and the proximity of Merida which provides culture, great restaurants, and US stores and restaurants to alleviate any home sickness.

"We primarily socialize with other English-speaking expats. We don't really integrate with other local residents other than hiring them to do work. The locals are amazing! They are friendly, happy, and always willing to help.

"Neither one of us spoke a word of Spanish before moving here. We are learning very slowly but we get by with sign language, pictures, and Google Translate. You must have a smart phone to get by! We also rely on the kindness of friends and strangers when speaking Spanish can't be avoided.

"The quality of healthcare here is excellent. The US should have the healthcare they have here!

"Roy had a hip replaced. We had insurance so it only cost us about $1,000 USD, but even without it, the total cost would have only been $8,000. Compare that to the US where the deductible would have been higher, and without insurance it would have been over $30,000. Roy's orthopedic surgeon, one of the best in Merida, came to our house to check up on him and change his dressing a week after the surgery! Try getting that in the US.

"Mexico has three levels of health insurance. The lowest level is something like Medicaid, which is free, and provides HIV care for free to everyone regardless of income. However, you wouldn't want to use those hospitals for a surgery if you can avoid it. Family members are expected to take on all non-medical responsibilities like food, washing, providing and changing bed sheets etc.

"Then there is a state-run health insurance which costs about $300 a year and provides services similar to national health services in Canada or Europe.

"Finally, there is private insurance like AXA and MetLife Mexico which costs about $1,800 per year and covers using private hospitals which are more like nice hotels. We have MetLife which provides $100,000 emergency coverage when we are in the US or traveling.

"For the most part private insurance does not cover the cost of drugs, but the normal prices are on par with the deductibles in the states. Here is another great example. An asthma inhaler in the states with insurance costs about $4. Without insurance, it's $300. Here the normal price is $3.

Rob and Roy have several pieces of advice for anyone who is considering living in Mexico.

"It is hot and humid here. It is hot year-round. There may be a few cool weeks in January, but otherwise the heat does not let up. It's also very sunny and the sun makes the heat even worse. Books don't last in the humidity here.

"Coming here for a week or two from the frigid north is not the same as living in this heat day in and day out year-round. Some people don't mind the heat and there is air conditioning, but unless you are from Louisiana or south Florida, the heat and humidity will get to you! It is very important for people to understand that.

"Probably the single best piece of advice I would give (and unfortunately one that I did not listen to), is to rent and live here for a few months to a year before deciding to move here. That way you can experience everything first hand before being committed into anything.

It's always different to experience something first hand than to hear or read about it.

Safety

Mexico is often perceived as a high-crime nation, but the fact is that many areas of the country are as safe as any other country, including the US. There are crime-ridden, unsafe areas in the US too, after all.

Most of the serious crime in Mexico is related to drug trafficking. Most of the violence occurs along drug transportation routes and certain border cities. Most of it occurs within the drug gangs and in their interactions with law enforcement, although innocent bystanders are occasionally affected.

Visit the US State Department's website to learn which areas you should avoid. You should exercise awareness and common sense in most places you go in Mexico and in the world. Generally, if there are Level 4 restrictions (the most dangerous) in place for travel by US government employees, you should probably not travel or live there.

All of the cities mentioned in this chapter are in safe areas. There are numerous articles on the Internet which suggest places for expats to retire that are located in some of the most dangerous states (for example, Mazatlan and Ixtapa/Zihuatanejo). Always do your research.

As of 2019, Mexico may be headed for a recession. President Trump's trade and immigration battles appear to be taking a toll on Mexico's economy, as growth has slowed to near zero. Mexico is receiving less business investment as companies fear that Mexico's current leftist president may nationalize industries.

Immigrating to Mexico

Mexico welcomes US retirees, and offers two types of visas for you to consider.

First, as a US citizen, you can visit in Mexico for up to six months without a visa. This is great for research trips or for snowbird arrangements. Beyond that, you can take a short trip outside the country (a visa run) before your six months are up, then re-enter Mexico and the clock starts over.

If you are planning to live in Mexico for longer than six months but less than four years, you can opt for the Temporary Resident Visa, or Visa de Residente Temporal. This visa is initially issued for one year, then renewed annually for up to four years. Of course, you have to show that you have sufficient monthly income to reside there, which is 300 times the Mexican minimum daily wage, which is about $1,200 a month. Or, you can provide bank or investment account statements that show you have maintained an average balance of at least 5,000 times the Mexican minimum daily wage (about $20,000). A third option is to own property in Mexico that is worth approximately $207,000 or more.

When you have lived in Mexico for four consecutive years, you need to either leave the country or apply for permanent residency. However, the four years you lived in Mexico with your Temporary Resident Visa qualifies you for permanent residency – you just have to do the paperwork.

If you know that you plan to live in Mexico longer than four years and you are retired, you can bypass the temporary visa and immediately apply for a Permanent Resident Visa, or Visa de Residente Permanente. You are considered retired if you are receiving regular pension or retirement income in any amount, even $1. The monthly income requirements are higher, yet still doable. The monthly income requirement is 500 times the Mexican minimum daily wage, which currently works out to a little over $2,000 a month. Alternatively, you can provide proof of investments with an average monthly value that is 20,000 times the Mexican minimum daily wage, which is currently about $100,000.

There are many websites and articles on the Internet that contain advice and resources about moving to Mexico and living there. Two of the best are Mexperience and Expats in Mexico.

Rob and Roy own and operate Bears En La Playa, a small bed and breakfast on the beach in Chelem, Mexico, on the Yucatan peninsula. Visit www.bearsenlaplaya.com to learn more.

Chapter 33

Retiring to Central or South America

There is no shortage of websites and articles that entice you to retire to Latin America. They show beautiful pictures and extol the benefits of low cost of living, a relaxed pace of life, and places to explore.

Most of them don't bother to report on the significant downsides to living in many of these places. Three often-overlooked factors that you should be mindful of are the country's political history and current situation, its economy, and its safety risks, such as petty crime, violent political demonstrations, and drug trafficking, among other things.

Before moving anywhere, you should research information on the US State Department and CIA websites, and from credible mainstream news sources. Try to find Facebook groups and expat forums that have a lot of current engagement from people who live there.

While no one can foresee the future, you should be wary of countries that have repressive or authoritarian governments and fragile economies. Look for high debt, inflation indicators, and evidence of trade problems.

In this chapter, I will recommend five Latin American countries in addition to Mexico that would make good choices for retirement. But first, here are a few countries you may see mentioned in retirement articles that I would be very hesitant to recommend or move to.

Nicaragua

Many websites tout Nicaragua as a particularly attractive retirement destination, citing beautiful architecture and beaches, an extremely low cost of living, and easy requirements for obtaining a residency visa as major benefits.

Those articles were probably written prior to 2018.

In the spring of 2018, citizens began staging peaceful demonstrations to protest several actions by president Daniel Ortega. Government response was violent, leaving many demonstrators dead or injured. Violent protests have continued into 2019. Nicaragua is not a safe place to be.

Ortega is, for all practical purposes, an authoritarian dictator. His wife is the vice-president. He effectively controls the police and the legislative and judicial branches of government, eliminating checks and balances.

Nicaragua is the poorest country in Central America. They have long been dependent upon economic assistance from Venezuela, but that country is mired in turmoil and severe depression.

Due to the country's weak economic situation, its authoritarian government, and the very real potential for social unrest and violence, I cannot recommend Nicaragua as a retirement destination.

This underscores the need to gain a thorough understanding of a country's government, economy, and recent history before you move there.

Belize

Belize is also frequently mentioned as a desirable retirement destination, primarily because English is the official language. It also offers low cost of living, beautiful waterfronts with world-renown scuba diving, and relatively close proximity to the US.

As it turns out, although English is the official language, Belize has more native Spanish speakers than English speakers. Belize suffers from high unemployment, a growing trade deficit, and heavy foreign debt burden.

A quick glance at the State Department's webpage on Belize reveals that "Belize is rated high for crime and has one of the highest per capita murder rates in the world. Crime may occur anywhere in Belize, and criminals frequently target tourists, including those at resorts and on the roads and river ways. Crime, including sexual assault, armed robbery, and murder, remains high and is distributed evenly throughout the country."

So, Belize is probably not a good place to retire.

Colombia

Colombia has made significant progress in reducing the power and influence of the violent drug cartels, and the government has signed a peace accord with a major rebel group. The country has experienced a remarkable turnaround in the past several years, and Medellin, in particular, is showing up in a lot of articles and Best Places to Retire lists. It's one of the least expensive places to live comfortably in the world.

Unfortunately, some parts of the country are still beset with violence. Crime and the potential for internal terrorist attacks are still present in Bogota and, to a lesser extent, Medellin. As of late 2019, there are signs that the peace accord between the government and the rebel groups is breaking down. If you're interested in checking out Colombia as a retirement destination, proceed with caution. The country seems a little too risky these days for me to recommend it.

Argentina

Buenos Aires is a European-inspired, world-class city rich with art and culture. Further inland, the wine region surrounding Mendoza is beautiful. Argentina is a wonderful place to visit, although due to recent events, now may not be the best time.

Argentina is embroiled in both economic and political crisis. The stock market dropped nearly 50 percent in one day and the country is experiencing rapid inflation, prompting even middle-class residents to fear that they may no longer be able to afford everyday products as the value of the Argentine peso falls.[25]

---

[25] https://www.washingtonpost.com/business/2019/08/15/key-countries-are-verge-recession-driving-fears-us-could-follow/

Unfortunately, Argentina probably won't recover from its ongoing economic and political challenges any time soon, so it is a poor choice for a retirement destination.

Brazil

Brazil is once again mired in political turmoil. The country's former president was swept from office as a result of corruption scandals. Their current right-wing president is rolling back social progress and stoking nationalism fears. Brazil's economy is experiencing contractions as exports and domestic spending have been sluggish.

All of this is most unfortunate. Brazil is rich in culture and natural beauty, not to mention its world-famous beaches. While the situation in Brazil is not nearly as dire as Venezuela or Argentina, the country still has problems with crime, especially in the large cities. Plus, some areas of Brazil are expensive relative to the rest of Latin America. You will find fewer English speakers in Brazil, so learning Portuguese is practically a necessity.

In better times, Brazil could be an excellent place to retire – especially some of the coastal cities further south. But for the foreseeable future, probably not.

Now that I have covered several countries that would not be good places to retire, let's look at a few that are.

Costa Rica

Of all the countries in Central America, Costa Rica is arguably the most modern, developed, and stable nation and is one of the easiest for a North American or European to adjust to.

In 1948, Costa Rica abolished its military forces and directed the money it wasn't spending on the military into education and healthcare.

As a result, Costa Rica's education system is ranked 20th in the world.[26] The literacy rate in Costa Rica is 96 percent, the highest rate in

---

[26] Global Competitiveness Report 2013–14

Latin America and the Caribbean. Costa Rica has had computers in schools for many years, and international high-tech companies have campuses in Costa Rica to take advantage of their well-educated, technically skilled work force. English is required in schools. While Spanish is still the primary spoken language, many Ticos (as the people of Costa Rica call themselves) speak some English.

Costa Rica has a world-class healthcare system.

Costa Rica places heavy importance on environmental preservation and sustainability.

Despite being a small country, there is a lot of variety within its boundaries. San Jose, the capital and the only city of significant size, is modern. There are small resort towns dotting the coasts and mountains in the central areas, including Arenal, an active volcano.

Many expats choose San Jose as their place to live. With many American companies and many familiar American stores and restaurant brands, San Jose won't seem too much different than home.

However, living in a big city might not be what you want. Escazu, Santa Ana, and Heredia are suburbs that are close enough to San Jose that you can easily travel there when you need big city culture, entertainment, or amenities. Heredia is home to the National University of Costa Rica, so you would enjoy the benefits of a college town. Santa Ana and Escazu have been called the Beverly Hills of Costa Rica. About 70 percent of the population of Costa Rica lives in the Central Valley, where all of the above cities are located.

If you would prefer to live closer to the Pacific coast, several areas in the Guanacaste and Alajuela provinces in the northwest part of Costa Rica are popular with expats. In Guanacaste, check out Tamarindo, Nosara, and Lake Arenal. In Alajuela, consider the San Carlos canton and its capital city, Ciudad Quesada. If you want to live close to the beach, Playa Herradura and Jaco are popular with expats.

The influx of expats in recent years has driven the price of real estate up in areas that have become popular with expats, so Costa Rica has become more expensive than many other places in Latin America. It's still less expensive than the US.

Of course, not everything in Costa Rica is perfect. Inflation is now under control, but until several years ago the country experienced 10-12 percent inflation every year.

Many roads throughout the country are just two lanes, and may become muddy during rainy season. Rural areas are less developed. Internet access is inconsistent in some places.

The US State Department gives Costa Rica a Level 1 rating – the safest rating. While the government is stable and the country is not prone to organized crime, terrorism, or violent protests, petty theft including home and car burglaries and robbery can be a problem. San Jose's crime profile is similar to some US cities.

Costa Rica offers a Pensionado (retiree) visa. You must be able to show proof of income of at least $1,000 a month from a pension plan, Social Security, or other investment income source for either one person or a married couple. You would start with a Temporary Visa for the first three years, then you can apply for a Permanent Visa.

Equal marriage rights will begin in Costa Rica in May, 2020.

Panama

Panama is often cited as one of the top foreign retirement destinations due to its low cost of living, close relationship with the US, the ease of securing a residency visa, and its enticing Pensionado program benefits.

Panama has enjoyed close relations with the United States for decades, primarily stemming from the US participation in building the Panama Canal. The Panama Canal Zone was a US possession until it was returned to Panama in 1999. Panama's currency, the Balboa, is pegged 1:1 with the US dollar. US currency is widely accepted.

You can qualify for a Pensionado Visa with a minimum monthly income of $1,000. That number drops to $750 if you purchase property worth at least $100,000.

In addition to residency, as a Pensionado you will enjoy these benefits:

- Import up to $10,000 worth of household goods tax-free
- 25 percent off flights (domestic and international) on some ticket categories
- 50 percent off entertainment (sporting events, movies, theatre, concerts)
- 30 percent off public transportation (bus, train, boat)

- 25 percent off utilities (electrical, telephone, and water)
- 50 percent reduction in home loan closing costs
- 10 percent discount on prescription medications
- 20 percent off on visits to the doctor and surgical procedures
- 15 percent discount on ophthalmic services
- 15 percent discount on dental procedures
- 25 percent discount at restaurants, although not all restaurants may honor this
- 15 percent discount at fast food restaurants
- 50 percent discount at hotels from Monday through Thursday, and 30 percent discount on weekends
- 15 percent off loans issued in the name of the retiree
- Special express lines for retirees at all banks in Panama

This is a permanent residency visa which does not expire. However, under this visa you cannot become a Panamanian citizen or work.

The mountain town of Boquete is particularly popular with expats. At almost 4,000 feet elevation, it has a year-round average temperature of about 65°F, which is considerably cooler than seaside locations. With the high concentration of expats, it's a good place for non-Spanish speakers to start their acclimation process. While Boquete is large enough to provide everything you need for daily living, it is a 7-hour drive to Panama City.

For seaside living, consider City Beaches, about an hour outside of Panama City. This area has been largely developed, which can be a plus or a minus depending on what you're looking for. It is home to thousands of expats from around the world, and has modern shopping and varied entertainment options. It's one of the more expensive areas of Panama, relatively speaking, but is still affordable compared to many other places in the world.

The cost of living varies widely in Panama, ranging from $1,000 to $8,000 a month for two. Cost of living is determined by factors such as how remote a place is and how much it is or is not developed. Places such as Boquete, City Beaches, and Panama City have become more expensive as they have grown in demand, due to the influx of expats. The plus side is that these places have more shopping and entertainment amenities and more new, modern homes geared towards people moving in from other countries. The downside is that it has driven prices up.

Claims that you can live in places like Panama for $1,500 a month no longer apply to these highly developed expat hotspots.

Overall, Panama is safe. Petty theft and opportunity crime are present in larger cities, as they are in most every country.

Same-sex marriage is not legal, and no form of civil union exists. Foreign same-sex marriages are recognized and marriage equality might be forthcoming following the Inter-American Court of Human Rights (IACHR) ruling and as a result of a case that is currently before Panama's Supreme Court.

Ecuador

Ecuador is frequently touted as one of the best destinations for retirement abroad. The cost of living is very cheap and the weather is consistent year-round.

Ecuador welcomes retirees and offers a Pensioner visa. This visa is easy to obtain, although the process can take up to 8 weeks. You need a monthly income of at least $800. A unique requirement of Ecuador's visa is that that you can only leave the country for up to 90 days total in each of the first two years. After that, you can be gone up to 18 months at a time.

Ecuador uses the US dollar as its currency. This means that you don't have to deal with currency exchange fees and you don't have to worry about fluctuations in the exchange rate.

The most popular retirement destination is Cuenca, a European-influenced inland city in the southern part of the country, located in the Andes mountains 8,400 feet above sea level. Expats who live in Cuenca report that there are many great restaurants, plenty of free concerts of many varieties, and art festivals. It's easy to get around and a new trolley system is replacing diesel buses.

The weather is pleasant year-round, with average highs of 70°F and average lows of 50°F. Some afternoons will be rainy during January through April. You will need very little heating and no air conditioning.

With 330,000 people, Cuenca is large enough to offer everything you need, but not so large that it has big-city problems. Ecuador's two largest cities, Guayaquil and Quito, are better suited to expats who are still working, but most retirees are attracted to Cuenca.

Loja, farther south, is a city of 180,000 in the beautiful Cuxibamba valley. Its year-round temperature range is slightly wider than Cuenca's with average highs of about 75°F and lows around 45°F. Loja holds a rich tradition in the arts, and for this reason is known as the Music and Cultural Capital of Ecuador. The city is home to two major universities.

If you prefer a smaller town, Cotacachi, in northern Ecuador, and Vilcabamba, in southern Ecuador, are idyllic smaller towns with a growing expat presence. They are close enough to larger cities (Quito and Loja, respectively) that you can travel there easily when you need to.

If you prefer to live near the ocean, there are numerous small towns dotting the coastline, and a couple mid-sized cities like Manta and Salinas. Each has its own charm and personality, but most do not have noticeable expat communities. If you move to one of these places, you will need to know Spanish and blend in with the locals. People who live there report that the locals are friendly and welcoming.

Whereas the cities and towns in the mountainous regions have spring-like weather year-round, along the coast the temperatures are hotter and there's less rain. The mountain cities have culture, Spanish architecture, restaurants with cuisines from around the world, shopping, and other modern amenities. The beach towns, on the other hand, tend to be more laid-back and less developed. Prices are generally higher on the coast than in the mountains.

Since travel within Ecuador is inexpensive, the most practical solution may be to live in Cuenca or one of the other cities mentioned above and travel to the beach whenever you feel like going.

Imported items in Ecuador are very expensive. If you hope to live inexpensively in Ecuador, you will need to purchase local goods.

Every first-hand account I have read from people living in Ecuador states that the Ecuadorian people are very friendly and welcoming. As with most of the rest of Latin America, the pace here is slower and people are much less stressed.

You will be happiest in Ecuador if you are willing to learn to speak fluent Spanish and adapt to their standard of living and their culture and environment.

Uruguay

The small South American country of Uruguay, nestled between Argentina and Brazil, may be one of the world's best kept secrets as a destination for both retirement and vacation travel.

Uruguay offers First World living at prices that are lower than many people in North America, Europe, Australia, and New Zealand are accustomed to paying. Uruguay is more expensive than many places in Latin America, but still quite affordable.

Uruguay is one of the most politically, socially, and economically stable countries in South America. Uruguay has modern, up-to-date infrastructure, including high-speed Internet and phone system, safe drinking water throughout the country, and high-quality medical care at inexpensive prices.

Uruguay has a year-round pleasant climate, although the humidity can be high (ranging from 50 to 100 percent) and it's often windy. It gets cold in the winter (July-August), but not cold enough for snow. It is not prone to natural disasters such as hurricanes or earthquakes.

Uruguay is remarkably safe. While there is some petty theft in Montevideo, violent crimes such as murder, personal assault, and robbery are rare and there is very little crime outside of Montevideo.

If you are considering moving to Uruguay, learning Spanish is essential. English is not widely spoken. The people are friendly and eager to help, but they can only help if they can understand you. Spanish in Uruguay is closer to the old-world Spanish spoken in Spain than the Mexican or Tex-Mex Spanish that some Spanish courses may teach. There is some overlap, but some difference as well.

The cities, Montevideo in particular, have European-influenced architecture and charm. 90 percent of the citizens have Spanish, French, or Italian ancestry. The beef in Uruguay is exceptionally good, as are the local wines. As a result, a large percentage of the meat you'll find in restaurants and grocery stores is beef. If you're not a red meat eater, you may be disappointed by the range of options available to you.

There are many fine restaurants and an active nightlife. Montevideo offers a range of live performance options. The national ballet, opera, and chamber orchestra all perform in the modern Auditorio Nacional Adela Reta (Adela Reta National Auditorium) with seating for 2,000.

You will also find electronic music, jazz, and rock playing in Montevideo nightclubs, small theaters, and bars.

The people are laid-back, friendly, well-educated, and polite. Uruguayan society is very egalitarian with a large middle class, in contrast to many other places in Latin America where there is noticeable income inequality and many people live in poverty. Former President Jose Mujica, who claims to have never worn a tie in his life, had no possessions other than a small farm and an old car. Current president Tabaré Vasquez is a physician who continues to work in his medical practice part-time.

There are beautiful beaches right in Montevideo, and most of Uruguay's coastline is lined with beaches. The ultimate Uruguay beach town is Punta del Este. For years, Punta has been the destination of choice for the rich and famous of Latin America and Europe, but it's still accessible to the middle class. Punta del Este is beautiful, clean, well-maintained, and very safe. There are palm trees, gleaming condo towers, and single-family homes with trim lawns. Outside Punta, the rolling hills of Maldonado are serene and picturesque.

Given its clientele, real estate in Punta del Este is predictably higher than Montevideo or anywhere else in the country. However, condos in the $100,000-$200,000 price range can be found. An interesting characteristic about Punta's real estate market is that price is determined more by the newness of the building and the amenities, not so much by location. So, you might find a $150,000 condo a short distance from million-dollar-plus residences. The town of La Barra, next to Punta del Este, is a good choice to consider since you would have proximity to Punta del Este, but with lower prices and fewer tourists.

The population and the activity noticeably surge during high season (January-February). During the off-season, it can be pretty quiet. There's plenty of art and culture to be found as well. Punta del Este has several modern art museums and hosts an international jazz festival every year.

I always caution people about moving full-time to beach towns and other resort locations. They are seductive and fun places to visit, but not necessarily a good place to live year-round. In this regard, Montevideo is probably the better choice for a permanent retirement destination, while you can easily drive a couple hours to Punta del Este for a week or a weekend.

Based on cost-of-living comparisons on Numbeo.com, the overall cost to maintain a comparable standard of living in Montevideo is comparable to less expensive areas of the US, such as the Midwest. Cost of living in Punta del Este is a bit higher.

Health insurance costs about $51 a month. Income tax rates are very reasonable (10-25 percent) and are only paid on income generated in Uruguay over $12,000 a year. That means that your retirement income is not taxed by Uruguay. (It's still taxed by the US, of course.) Value-Added Tax (VAT) is fairly high, but it's included in the sticker price of everything you buy. Uruguay places stiff import taxes on goods from outside the country, which may be why income taxes are so low.

Prices in Uruguay are higher than in most other places in Latin America, yet still reasonable by world standards. If low-cost living is a high priority, this may not be the place for you. Given the high quality of healthcare, infrastructure, and overall quality of life, I think Uruguay is an appealing option to consider.

It's relatively easy to get a foreign retiree visa. To qualify, you must have a documented retirement income of at least $1,500 per month. The country allows you to move your household possessions, including one car, into the country without being taxed. Uruguay is also pet-friendly and there is no quarantine period once you arrive with your pet.

One of the main disadvantages of living in Uruguay is that travel to and from the US can be lengthy and expensive, and currently the only direct flight from Montevideo to the US flies into Miami. However, Uruguay is close to Buenos Aires, Argentina, so you'll have more options for travel to and from that city. Other connections are available through Santiago, Chile and Panama City.

Uruguay was the first South American country to institute civil unions, and the second to institute same-sex marriage (after Argentina). Punta del Este, the main seaside resort in Uruguay, has a tradition of being one of the most gay-friendly tourist destinations in Latin America.

Chile

Chile is one of the most stable, prosperous, and safest countries in Latin America. The government is not corrupt and people are generally honest. The infrastructure is excellent. Chile is First World by any standard. Consequently, it is not as cheap to live there in comparison with most other Latin American countries.

Chile has a world-class healthcare system. Their public and private systems provide care that is comparable to what you would receive in North America and Europe. The last World Health Organization rankings placed Chile five places ahead of the United States.

Santiago's steady economic growth over the past few decades has transformed it into a modern metropolis. The city is now home to a growing theater and restaurant scene, extensive suburban development, dozens of shopping centers, and a rising skyline. Temperatures range from the mid-60s to the mid-80s during the dry summer (December through February) and from the mid-30s to the mid-50s in the wetter winter.

Santiago is surrounded by mountains, so air pollution is a problem. The entire country is prone to earthquakes, although buildings are built to withstand them.

Aside from the pollution in Santiago, Chile is clean and safe. The tap water is safe to drink. There is less poverty in Chile than in many other Latin American countries.

Chileans are friendly, but they socialize primarily with their families. Many expats report that integrating into their social circles and forming close friendships is very challenging.

So far, the country doesn't have a large expat population, probably due to the relatively higher cost of living. About 51,000 English-speaking expats live throughout the country, primarily from the UK and South Africa. There are no communities or suburbs that have become magnets for expats like you would find in Mexico, Panama, or Ecuador.

Aside from Santiago, there are a few other places that attract expats. The oceanside cities of La Serena and Coquimbo (about 5 hours north of Santiago, combined population 350,000) offers six miles of beaches and good shopping. La Serena is safer and less expensive than Santiago. Viña del Mar (vineyard by the sea) is a wealthy resort city with beautiful gardens, palm-lined boulevards, museums, and nightlife. It's near Valparaiso and less than two hours from Santiago. Farther south, in the Lakes region, picturesque smaller towns such as Puerto Veras and Pucón are set among beautiful lakes with stunning mountain views, offering plentiful outdoor activities in a cooler climate.

Chile does not have a visa that is specific to retirees, but retirees are eligible to follow the same process for obtaining a visa as anyone else. Chile requires no minimum financial investment, but when you apply for permanent residency you are required to provide proof that you can support yourself.

First, obtain a Temporary Visa (Visa Temporario) which is valid for one year. You can arrive first on a Tourist Visa, then apply for a Temporary Visa once you're there.

Before your one-year Temporary Visa expires, you must either renew it for one year or proceed to apply for permanent residency (Permanencia Definitiva). A Temporary Visa may only be renewed once, and you must be present in the country to do so. The permanent visa is renewable every five years, indefinitely.

After having permanent residency for five years, you are eligible to apply for Chilean citizenship. You can hold dual citizenship.

Chapter 34

Retiring to Europe

Europe is a wonderful continent, with many charming cites, stunning architecture, rich history and culture, and excellent public transportation – both within cities and for travel across Europe.

Unfortunately, many countries in Europe do not offer a retirement visa. If you are not married to a citizen of the country you wish to relocate to, you can only receive a visa for work, study, or reunification with immediate family.

Some countries, such as Germany and Austria, do not have a retirement visa per se, but they are less strict about the requirement for work, study, or family reunification. You can qualify for a visa if you can demonstrate that you have sufficient income to support yourself. The amount varies by country.

At this time, to the best of my knowledge and research to date, the countries that offer visas for retirees are Portugal, Spain, Andorra, France, Italy, Malta, Greece, Croatia, and Cyprus. There may be others. If you have your heart set on a particular country, you can dig deeper into the visa requirements for that country.

Note some of the above countries require proficiency in the country's official language as a condition of receiving a permanent residency visa, which you can apply for after living in the country for five years on a temporary visa. Countries with a language requirement are Austria, Germany, Italy, Croatia, and possibly others.

If you are determined to live permanently in a European Union country other than one of those listed above, your best path might be to immigrate to one of the above countries first, gain citizenship (which will usually take five years or more), then move to the country of your dreams. Once you are a citizen of an EU nation, you may live in any other EU nation as long as you have health insurance coverage in your host country and sufficient income to live without government support.

If you are interested in retiring in Europe or traveling extensively there, you should understand several of the legal agreements and relationships that exist among European countries. There's the European Union (EU), the European Economic Area (EEA), and the Schengen Area (named after the city in Luxembourg where this agreement was signed).

The European Union (EU) is a political and economic union of 28 countries, currently. That list may expand in the future, and the United Kingdom is in the process of leaving the EU ("Brexit").

As of October, 2019, the members of the EU are Austria, Belgium, Bulgaria, Croatia, Cyprus, the Czech Republic (Czechia), Denmark, Estonia, Finland, France, Germany, Greece, Hungary, Ireland, Italy, Latvia, Lithuania, Luxembourg, Malta, the Netherlands, Poland, Portugal, Romania, Slovakia, Slovenia, Spain, Sweden, and the United Kingdom. Other territories that are owned by any of these nations are also part of the EU, such as French Guiana and French Polynesia.

The nations that are part of the Schengen Area are: Austria, Belgium, the Czech Republic, Denmark, Estonia, Finland, France, Germany, Greece, Hungary, Iceland, Italy, Latvia, Liechtenstein, Lithuania, Luxembourg, Malta, the Netherlands, Norway, Poland, Portugal, Slovakia, Slovenia, Spain, Sweden, and Switzerland.

Note that this list does not completely align with the list of nations that comprise the EU. Nations that are in the EU but not part of the Schengen Area are Bulgaria, Croatia, Cyprus, Ireland, Romania, and the United Kingdom. Nations that are part of the Schengen Area but not members of the EU are Iceland, Liechtenstein, Norway, and Switzerland.

The important distinction here is that the Schengen Area provides for easy travel among these countries, while the EU provides residency rights for citizens of other EU countries.

The Schengen Area is relevant to all travelers from non-Schengen nations, because you are allowed to remain in the Schengen Area for up to 90 days in any 180-day period. For example, if you spend 90 days in Spain, you can't immediately spend the next 90 days in France. You must leave the Schengen Area for at least 90 days before you return to any country in the Schengen Area.

The European Economic Area (EEA) is basically the EU plus Norway, Iceland, and Lichtenstein. At a high level, the EEA aims to ensure the free movement of goods, services, people, and capital among the member countries. Since these three nations are part of the Schengen Area, that covers the travel aspect. The EEA appears to confer residency rights as the EU does.

As the United Kingdom prepares to leave the EU, many details concerning residency and travel are still to be determined. The UK may remain in the EEA. It appears that agreements are being worked out which will prevent citizens of other EU nations currently living in the UK from having to leave, as well as UK citizens who are currently living in other EU nations.

Citizens of Scotland, the majority of whom voted against Brexit, may vote to secede from the UK and petition to join the EU as a sovereign nation.

Several other nations are currently in various stages of applying for membership in the EU.

The bottom line is that the situation in Europe is in flux, and the possibilities for retiring in Europe may change too.

In the next few chapters, I will highlight several countries that are good retirement choices. These are by no means the only places to retire in Europe, so if you have your heart set on some other country, do your research using some of the websites on the Resources page. There are plenty of articles with stories from expats which will give you more insight into both the good and bad aspects of living in any given place.

Portugal

If you dream of retiring to Europe, Portugal is well worth your consideration. It is the least expensive country in Western Europe, its immigration requirements can be satisfied by most retirees, and the country enjoys mild, sunny weather.

Portugal has long been a favorite of expats from Great Britain and other European countries, but it has only recently begun to attract more attention from people in the US and Canada.

Low cost of living is not the only benefit Portugal offers. It also offers beautiful landscapes and architecture. The Algarve region at the southern end of Portugal boasts some of the best beaches in Europe. High-speed Internet is available in 90 percent of the country and 4G service in 95 percent. Portugal has been rated the 17th safest country in the world.

Portugal's location at the southwest corner of the European continent means that you will have to travel farther to reach destinations beyond Spain, but you can still travel freely to most of the rest of Europe. Once you become a resident of Portugal, you can travel visa-free to all 26 European countries in the Schengen Area.

English is widely spoken in the Algarve, and to a lesser extent in Lisbon and Porto, and not so much in the more rural areas. Expats report that it is easier to make friends in Portugal than in many other expat destinations, and it is easier to get by with English while you are coming up to speed on Portuguese. Cultural adaptation seems to be easier in Portugal than in many places.

The most frequently heard complaints about living in Portugal are the government bureaucracy and the very lengthy time it takes merchandise ordered overseas to make it through customs. It could take months.

Three areas are particularly worthy of your consideration: Lisbon, Porto, and the Algarve. Aside from these three, there are numerous mid-sized cities along the coast from Lisbon to Porto that seem charming.

Lisbon

Lisbon is Portugal's largest city, its capitol, and the country's hub for business and finance. If you prefer living in a larger city for the wider range of activities and the cultural amenities it has to offer, Lisbon would be your best choice.

If you prefer suburban living, Cascais is located on the coast just west of Lisbon. Many expats have located here. Suburbs such as Cascais offer more room and less bustle than Lisbon, but it's just a 30-minute train ride into the city when you want to go there. Cascais is the most expensive place (relatively speaking), so you might consider towns like Oeiras, Parede, and Caixas, which are on the same train line but more affordable.

If your plans call for exploring the rest of Europe, you will be able to do this most conveniently if you are based in or near Lisbon, because you will be close to the airport. You can find inexpensive, frequent flights to most other cities in Europe.

Porto

If you prefer a medium-sized city, Porto, in the northern region of Portugal, is worth checking out. It's also the center of Portugal's wine region and the namesake of Port wine.

The city features stunning architecture and old-world charm, but there are also areas with new development. Interestingly, the older properties with character are being bought up by expats while the locals are migrating to the newer developments. There are numerous smaller towns near Porto, both along the coast and inland, where housing prices are lower and the pace is more relaxed.

The Algarve

The Algarve is the southernmost region of Portugal, and it's the region that has attracted the most attention as a retirement destination. It's the sunniest and warmest spot on the European continent. The 100-mile coastline offers beautiful beaches, plentiful golf courses, and spectacular cliffs and caves. There are no large cities, only a string of smaller oceanfront towns such as Faro, Lagos, Portimao, Ablufeira, and Tavira.

This region has long been a tourist destination for the rest of Europe, especially England, so you would have to contend with the influx of tourists during summer vacation season. Some expats feel that the

Algarve is too touristy in the summer and dead in the winter. Because of its history as a vacation destination, English is widely spoken here.

Climate

The climate and weather in Portugal are usually excellent, generally being neither too hot nor too cold. The climate varies from north to south and from the coast to inland regions, but in general Portugal offers warm and sunny summers, mild winters, and pleasant but rainy autumns and springs.

In the northern region, including Porto, the summers are sunny and pleasantly warm without becoming sweltering hot. Further inland, where it's more mountainous, the winters are colder than in the rest of Portugal, with occasional snowfall in the Serra da Estrela Mountains.

The central region of Portugal, including Lisbon, experiences a combination of elements from the Mediterranean and Atlantic climate which means mild winters and hot and dry summers. The inner regions of central Portugal can get very hot during the summer with temperatures over 85°F, whereas the coastal areas are cooled by ocean breezes.

In the Algarve, summers are particularly dry and sunny with 12 hours of sunshine each day and an average temperature range of 68-82°F.The constant sea breeze helps to keep temperatures at pleasant levels.

Cost of Living

The cost of living in Portugal is, on average, 30 percent lower than in any other country in Western Europe. A retired couple could live frugally on a budget of as little as $1,500 per month, and live quite comfortably on a budget of $2,000 a month.

Prices are highest in Lisbon, particularly for rent, but prices are still about 80 percent of the US midpoint. Almost everything is cheaper, especially once you leave the tourist areas. The only items that are significantly more expensive in Lisbon are automobiles ($8-10,000 higher), gasoline (200 percent higher), and the cost to buy (not rent) an apartment. Given that public transportation is good, you could easily get by without a car.

Surprisingly, the cost of living in the Algarve is still remarkably low, even compared to the rest of Portugal. Prices in Faro, for example, are 16 percent lower than Lisbon. The overall cost of living is just 70 percent of the US average. You would probably be more inclined to own a car in this region, so you might need to factor the costs of gasoline and car ownership into your budget.

Fortunately, you'll get a tax break if you move to Portugal. Any income from pensions, Social Security, and other foreign sources (such as your investments) will be free from local taxes for ten years if your home country has a double-taxation treaty with Portugal, as the United States, Canada, and the United Kingdom do.

Healthcare

Portuguese healthcare was ranked by World Health Organization as the 12th best system in the world, out of 190 countries. The United States ranked 37th, by comparison.

Like most European countries, Portugal has two separate healthcare systems – a publicly financed National Health Service that is available to all citizens, along with a private healthcare network available on a fee basis, which is what non-citizens would use. Expats in Portugal should purchase international health insurance; in fact, it is required for visa applications.

Doctors are generally trained to North American or European standards, and many speak English, especially in the tourist destinations.

Ease of Immigration

Portugal welcomes immigrants and their requirements for visas and permanent residence are low enough for most retirees to meet.

The process and the paperwork can be lengthy and tedious, but it's doable. You will benefit from hiring a reputable immigration attorney who knows the process thoroughly and can ensure that the process runs smoothly.

You can qualify for permanent residency in Portugal simply by showing a reliable income, either earned or passive, of at least €1,100 per month. This requirement is not specific to retirees; you can apply and qualify at any age. To maintain residency status, you must be physically present in the country for 183 days or more every year.

Portugal also offers a Golden Visa program, in which you qualify for residency by buying real estate. The required investment amount ranges from €500,000 to as little as €280,000 for a renovation project in an identified low-density or depressed region. Under the Golden Visa program, you only need to be present in the country for a minimum of one or two weeks a year.

Of course, it's not a good idea to buy real estate in a foreign country before you have lived there for at least a year. You will want to be sure that you are going to enjoy living there, and you will need time to explore various places to live, become familiar with local laws and prices, and establish relationships with reputable realtors, attorneys and financial institutions.

Once you have been a legal resident for six years, you can apply for Portuguese citizenship. This will open the door to moving elsewhere in Europe, if that's your ultimate goal. The US and Portugal allow dual citizenship.

Spain

For many years, Spain has enjoyed a reputation as a fantastic vacation destination. Its warm climate, sunny Mediterranean beaches, history, art, and culture, as well as its friendly, easy-going, relaxed atmosphere, have delighted travelers for years.

Spain is a popular retirement choice, especially for people from the United Kingdom. There are approximately 300,000 Britons (working and retired) living in Spain, along with 43,000 from the US and 7,000 from Canada. All told, expats make up about one of every eight people in Spain.

The Climate

If warm weather is your preference, you'll find most of Spain to your liking, especially along the Mediterranean coast. Summers there are hot but not oppressive. Malaga, a coastal city in the south, records average highs of 30°C (86°F) in summer. Temperatures rarely dip below freezing in Barcelona, at the north end of the coast; coastal cities farther south never experience freezing temperatures, and it never snows.

Madrid, in central Spain, gets very hot in summer. It's slightly hotter and more humid than the coast, and may see below-freezing temperatures and snowfall in winter. Spring and fall bring heavy rains.

The northern (Atlantic) coast of Spain is the coolest and rainiest. However, it's is also the greenest. Bilbao is an attractive, welcoming city that would be a good choice if you prefer this climate.

Sevilla, the largest city in the southern Andalusia region, is about an hour inland, and its climate is comparable to that of Phoenix, Arizona – hot, but dry.

The climate of the Canary Islands remains remarkably constant and very pleasant year-round. Temperatures average 18-24°C (64-75°F) throughout the year. The easternmost islands are semi-arid, while the westernmost islands receive more rainfall. The islands claim to have the most ideal climate in the world, and if you like your weather warm and relatively dry, it would be hard to argue.

Cost of Living

Here's where most of Spain excels, in comparison with the rest of Western Europe. Only Portugal offers a cost of living that is cheaper than Spain. Compared to France, Italy, Germany, the UK and Scandinavia, Spain is a bargain.

Madrid and Barcelona are Spain's two largest cities and offer the most in the way of culture, entertainment, and socialization opportunities. With so much to offer, they are popular and therefore expensive, and may be less favorable to retirees for whom lower cost of living is a concern. Compared to the US average cost of living, average costs are 15 percent higher in Madrid and 9 percent higher in Barcelona. If you're accustomed to living in one of the more expensive US cities, cost of living in Madrid or Barcelona will seem comparable or perhaps slightly cheaper.

When you leave these two large cities, prices drop considerably. The most noticeable price difference is the cost to rent or buy your home. Most of Spain's other large cities, such as Valencia, Malaga, and Sevilla, are statistically similar to each other.

In general, the costs of restaurant dining, soda, dairy, and meat are slightly higher in Spain. Gasoline, cars, some leisure activities, clothes, and buying a home are considerably higher. Foods other than dairy and meat, beer, wine, local public transportation, and renting a home are usually lower. Rents are considerably higher in Barcelona and Madrid.

Taxes are somewhat higher; the federal tax rate ranges from 25 percent to 54 percent. A married couple with a combined annual income of €100,000 would pay around 33 percent, after deductions. If you live in Spain for at least half of the year, you are considered a Spanish resident for tax purposes, regardless of your visa or citizenship status.

Healthcare

As with many modern countries with tax-supported, socialized healthcare, healthcare in Spain is considerably less expensive than in the US. In terms of quality, Spain's healthcare system was rated 7th best in the world, according to the often-referenced World Health Organization's 2000 study.

Free public healthcare is available only to those who have been employed in Spain, and have therefore paid into the system. Most expat retirees will need to join a private healthcare system with private health insurance. Fortunately, this is reasonably priced, and there is a wide variety of plans from which to choose.

Quality of Living

In addition to the warm, sunny climate and the affordable cost of living, other factors contribute Spain's quality of life. While Barcelona and Madrid are certainly cultural hubs, other cities have plenty to offer too – especially Sevilla. There's the Picasso Museum in Malaga (his birthplace) and the Guggenheim in Bilbao. There are ancient castles to explore all over the country. And there are beautiful beaches up and down the Mediterranean coast.

Many of Spain's cities would make good retirement choices, especially those along the Mediterranean coast and Sevilla, which is about an hour's drive inland. Each region of Spain has its own distinctive qualities in terms of historical influence, topography, culture, and climate.

The Canary Islands offer nearly ideal weather and reasonable cost of living, and there is an abundance of natural beauty and plenty to explore around the seven major islands. Each of the islands is different in terms of what it has to offer, but bear in mind that you will be living on a somewhat isolated island chain.

Throughout Spain, people are relaxed. In Spain, the emphasis is on enjoying food and wine, relaxing, socializing, and just enjoying life. After all, this is the country that brought us paella, tapas, gazpacho, and sangria.

Like anywhere else, Spain is not perfect and not everyone has a pleasant expat experience in Spain. People often complain about slow and inattentive service, crushing bureaucracy, dishonest business dealings, and crime – although crime statistics on Numbeo.com look pretty good. Some folks have experienced bias directed towards anyone who is not Spanish.

Immigrating to Spain

If you are a citizen of another European Union nation, it is easy to move to Spain. For residents of non-EU countries, you'll need a visa.

For a resident visa, the application process is tedious and bureaucratic, but doable. As long as you can prove that you have sufficient financial resources, no criminal record, and you purchase private health insurance coverage, you should be able to get your visa.

France

Most Best Places to Retire websites and articles include France at or near the top of their lists.

It's easy to see why: the scenery is beautiful, the country is rich in culture and full of things to see and do, and the cuisine and wine are among the best in the world. Although the country is geographically diverse, most areas of the country enjoy a very pleasant climate throughout most of the year.

France is not one of those places you're likely to consider if you are seeking a substantially lower cost of living, although you will save a lot of money on healthcare. You are more likely to find France appealing if you are looking for quality of life, history, culture, and delicious food and wine.

France's healthcare system has been rated the best in the world. French medical schools are among the best in the world, hence so are the doctors. France has one of the highest ratios of doctors to patients, and most doctors are fluent in English. Office visits are inexpensive, and most procedures are almost fully covered with only a tiny co-pay. Of course, out-of-pocket costs are so low because the rest is covered by taxes, which can total as much as 40 percent.

If you are a property owner in France, you qualify to participate in their healthcare system. Otherwise, you will need private health medical insurance when you retire there, which costs about $1,500 per person, per year. You can look into reducing costs by buying insurance as a member of a larger group or association, which can reduce the premiums by as much as 50 percent.

Of course, when you think of France, you think of Paris. It's truly a world-class city, full of things to experience and explore. It's also the most expensive place to live in France, but if you are relatively well-off and thrive on big city living, it might be the place for you. You can still live there affordably if you find a place away from the most popular areas. You won't need a car in Paris, since public transportation can take you almost anywhere.

The Languedoc-Roussillon region hugs the curve of the Mediterranean coastline, closer to Spain. Languedoc offers the same beauty, charm, and balmy weather as the more famous and fashionable Marseille or Nice to the east, but with fewer crowds, less gloss, and at half the price. Whereas the ritzy resorts of the Cote d'Azur attract the wealthy and famous, Languedoc has charming little hotels, long sandy beaches, Roman aqueducts, and is home to artists and writers. From Montpellier, the region's largest city, you can travel to Paris, Barcelona, or Marseille in less than three hours. Real estate is still very affordable, especially if you move inland from the coast. The area boasts 300 days of sunshine a year, mild winters, and hot but not oppressive summers.

Bordeaux offers warmer summers and winters, so it is more likely to rain than snow. It's a popular expat destination where you'll find immigrants from Spain, Portugal, North Africa, the UK, Ireland, and the Netherlands. As such, you're more likely to find English speakers here. Provence is another area that is popular with expats.

France offers a retiree visa. Most information I have found does not indicate a specific amount of income that you need to demonstrate, but since France can be expensive you should expect that to be fairly high.

Malta

If warm, sunny weather, reasonable cost of living, and excellent yet inexpensive healthcare are among your top criteria for selecting a place to retire, Malta might be just what you're looking for. Malta is a tiny island nation located in the middle of the Mediterranean Sea, just 58 miles (93 km) south of Sicily and 241 miles (388 km) east of Tunisia.

Not surprisingly, Malta is one of the sunniest and warmest places in Europe. It rarely rains in May through August, but about one-third of the days in the winter months see some rain. Winter low temperatures will occasionally dip below 50°F (10°C), while summer highs rarely exceed 93°F (34°C). Humidity is fairly high, ranging from 65 percent in July to 80 percent in December.

Its population is about 475,000, and its total size is 122 square miles (316 square km). That's about the same size and population as Atlanta, Georgia. So, imagine Atlanta being an island nation, and that's Malta. Since English is one of Malta's two official languages and it has among the easiest immigration requirements in Europe, Malta might be well worth your consideration.

I had the opportunity to visit Malta, albeit for only one day, as part of a Mediterranean cruise. I found the capital city of Valletta and the neighboring countryside to be attractive and charming. It is one of the world's oldest recorded civilizations and is home to nine UNESCO World Heritage sites. Valletta exudes 16th century charm, yet still feels like a modern, vibrant city.

The Republic of Malta consists of three islands. The main island is also called Malta (93 square miles). Gozo (26 square miles) is located a 25-minute ferry ride to the northwest, and tiny Comino (1.4 square miles) lies between the two.

Gozo's population is just over 37,000. It's much less densely populated than Malta island, and features numerous beaches and resorts. It's also considered one of the top diving destinations in the Mediterranean.

Comino has a population of 3 and is primarily a bird sanctuary and nature preserve.

Although Malta is lovely and offers many benefits, it's not paradise. It has its problems and downsides, which this chapter will cover.

What's Great About Malta

Malta has both a public healthcare system and a private healthcare system. Public healthcare is free for Malta residents and EU citizens, including a full range of treatments and medications. The quality of healthcare is excellent. The only problem with the public system is the wait times. If you are seeking non-life-threatening medical care, you could wait months for an appointment. Some people choose to pay for private care just to receive their care sooner.

Foreign residents are advised to obtain private health insurance, but this is extremely inexpensive. You can buy a simple in-patient plan for as low as €90 a year. Full coverage is available for around €350 a year, allowing you to see doctors at one of the many private clinics and hospitals in order to avoid the queues at public facilities.

Overall cost of living is only slightly higher than the US average, and lower than most other places in Europe. Predictably, gasoline is much higher, but because the island is so small, you won't be driving great distances. Since public transportation is available throughout the islands, you could easily get by without a car. Most other utilities are lower. Restaurant prices are only slightly higher, while grocery prices are slightly lower. Rent is slightly cheaper except in the most expensive areas, but prices to buy real estate are significantly higher.

Crime is very low, with the notable exception of government bribery and corruption. More on that below. Crime is practically non-existent on Gozo.

Ease of immigration is perhaps Malta's biggest selling point. It offers the easiest and fastest path to immigration in Europe.

Malta does not have a visa specifically designed for retirees, but it does offer a unique Global Residence Program for non-EU citizens. You can qualify by renting a place to live for as little as €800 per month. This is the only country in the EU that grants a residency visa for simply renting an apartment or house. You don't even have to live there the majority of the year.

Once you have a Malta residency visa, you have access to travel in the rest of the Schengen Area. For some countries with much more restrictive immigration policies, this offers your easiest and cheapest access. You also have access to Malta's free public healthcare, as discussed above.

Life in Malta is generally slow-paced and relaxed. The proximity to the sea from almost any point on the island and 300 days of sunshine is conducive to reduced stress and a pleasant retirement lifestyle. There are lots of community celebrations and colorful festivals.

For a nation of less than half a million people, Malta has a lot of culture to offer. There's an annual jazz festival, theatre, and many historical sites to discover. Malta was designated the Culture Capital of Europe for 2018.

What's Not So Great about Malta

On Malta island, roads are narrow and often poorly maintained. As the population has increased, so has the number of cars filling the roads and vying for limited parking spaces. Although there are buses that will take you almost anywhere, they have to sit in traffic too. During rush hours, the buses can be very full, and they might simply pass bus stops because they have no more room for passengers. This is not the case on Gozo, as you'll read below.

Since Malta has a history of being a haven for money laundering and other off-shore banking practices, you might be treated very suspiciously in your dealings with a bank. Some expats have experienced great difficulty just opening a bank account or getting a check book or debit card. Obtaining a credit card can be even more difficult. Others report less difficulty, so it's probably a combination of factors such as which bank you are using, what country you are from, your financial condition, and your credit score.

Pollution is worse in Malta than in the US and most of Europe. Water quality is very good, but air quality, litter, overall cleanliness, and garbage disposal complaints are worse. Dust blows in from nearby Africa, making it necessary to clean your home more frequently.

The relaxed pace of life has its downside as well. Service can be leisurely and wait times can be long. It's not uncommon for repair people to stand you up for a service appointment repeatedly.

Since Malta gained its independence from the United Kingdom in 1964, both of its ruling political parties have allegedly maintained very close ties to the island's most powerful families. The lines between police, justice, and business are often blurred. In addition to legitimate industries such as tourism and shipping, part of Malta's economic success has been based on off-shore financial services, tax avoidance models, shell companies, crypto-currencies, and online gambling. Various Maltese entities were implicated in the leaked Panama Papers.

Malta and Gozo are small islands, and living on an island isn't for everyone. Depending on your desires for entertainment, culture, and exploration, the small size of the island may feel restrictive. This will be especially true if you settle on Gozo.

If one of the reasons you want to retire to Europe is so that you can travel around the continent, the extensive train system is unavailable to you. Aside from taking a ferry to Sicily, you'll need to travel by airplane to reach anyplace else you want to go. Fortunately, direct flights to most of Europe's major airports are available several times a day for $250 or less, round trip.

If you live on Gozo, you'll need to add in travel to Malta island before you can take off for other places. The ferry ride from Gozo to Malta takes 25 minutes and the tickets are inexpensive, so traveling to the main island is not difficult.

Where to Live in Malta

Sliema, St. Julian's, and neighboring communities offer an abundance of restaurants, shopping, and services. These cities are the most cosmopolitan and fashionable areas of Malta. For this reason, the cost of living tends to be more expensive than elsewhere on the island. The nearby suburbs such as Gzira, Msida, Swieqi, and Ta Xbiex are less expensive yet still provide access to Sliema and St. Julian's.

The capital city of Valletta is an incredibly beautiful town which has preserved a lot of the medieval feel of its history, with its limestone buildings and fortress walls. Cars are not allowed in parts of the city, making it safe and pleasant (albeit hilly) for pedestrian traffic.

Valletta has an abundance of cafes, bars, and restaurants, but it is a cruise ship port and a focal point for historical places, so you can expect to see tourists nearly all year round. Valletta merits repeat visits to discover its history and enjoy its ambiance, but with a population of just under 7,000, it may not be the best place to live. If you are attracted to Valletta, the neighboring towns of Floriana and Pieta are good choices.

The central region of Malta, anchored by Birkirkara, is the most densely populated region on the island. The biggest advantages of living in the central area are lower cost of living, as well as the ease of reaching everywhere else on the island.

Mellieha, in the northwest corner of the island, is where you'll find a large number of villas, holiday homes, and beautiful beaches. Santa Maria Estate is popular with older expats, particularly Brits. Since it is quieter and more relaxed than the areas mentioned above, Mellieha can offer a more leisurely lifestyle for those not looking to go out a lot.

The island of Gozo is a lovely place which offers a calmer alternative to Malta island. The total population of Gozo is around 37,000, and the area is 67 square kilometers or 26 square miles, so the population density is about one-third of that on Malta island. The capital of Gozo, Victoria, is centrally located, and with a population of 7,000, it's the largest city on the island.

Cost of living on Gozo, including rent, is among the lowest in the country. The bus service on Gozo is better than on Malta, and nothing is more than 15 minutes away. The perimeter of the island is dotted with seaside villages such as Xlendi, Marsalforn and Mgarr. Gozo is more relaxed and crime is practically non-existent, but living on such a small island isn't for everybody.

Chapter 35

Retiring to Southeast Asia

Southeast Asia is among the cheapest places in the world to live. You often see a few countries or cities in this region mentioned on Best Places to Retire lists.

Four countries currently offer residency visas that retirees can avail themselves of: Thailand, Malaysia, Indonesia, and the Philippines. I can give a lukewarm recommendation only to Thailand. If you are considering retiring to any of the others, do a lot of research and plan an extended visit.

While it is cheap, the disadvantages of living in this region far outweigh the advantages, in my opinion.

Like most places in Asia, the cities are dense, crowded, and usually polluted. Traffic can be heavy and people drive in a much less disciplined manner, which takes some adjustment.

Asian countries may present more challenges for successful assimilation into the culture, especially for people from the Americas and Europe. Social customs are very different. Languages such as Chinese and Thai are difficult for westerners to learn since tonal inflection plays a more significant role.

Laws are different, too. Malaysia and Indonesia are Muslim-majority countries, and while their laws are not as strict as those in countries such as Saudi Arabia or Iran, they are still aligned with Islamic tenets. In some regards, there is a double standard applied to Muslims and non-Muslims. For example, alcohol may be sold in restaurants and bars, but only to non-Muslim patrons.

Homosexual activity is illegal in Malaysia, although laws are supposedly rarely enforced. Hotels have been known to report two unmarried people staying in the same hotel room to the government. Oddly, Malaysia now prohibits discrimination on the basis of sexual orientation or gender identity in employment.

Thailand is very tolerant on many issues, but you could be arrested for speaking anything negative about the monarchy. Thailand offers some legal protections for LGBT people including, as of early 2019, civil partnerships.

The Philippines is a reasonably tolerant country, too. It's the only country in Asia which is predominantly Christian (Catholic). However, the country is currently experiencing political unrest and an increase in crime and terrorism in some areas.

If you wish to consider Malaysia, check out Penang, an island in the northwest corner of the country. George Town, its largest city, is not as large as many Asian cities and is easy to navigate. Many multinational tech companies have campuses on the island, so there's more western influence and a larger expat population.

In Indonesia, the most popular destination for western expats is Bali. Bali is beautiful, popular with tourists, and religious and cultural restrictions are less prevalent. It's a popular spot for young digital nomads.

In Thailand, the most frequently recommended city for expats and retirees in Chiang Mai.

In the Philippines, it's Cebu.

Chapter 36

Retiring to New Zealand

New Zealand is my favorite country on the planet. It's beautiful and full of interesting places to explore and things to do. The people are friendly. It's serene and safe. Auckland is consistently listed among the world's most livable cities. Wellington and Dunedin are nice, too.

On the other hand, it's expensive. During my visit there, grocery prices were often twice what I'm used to paying in the US. Real estate is more expensive, too. Prices are highest in Auckland, but get cheaper as you move south. Dunedin is more affordable, but colder. Located near one of Earth's biggest fault lines, New Zealand is prone to earthquakes. Two serious earthquakes have devastated downtown Christchurch in the past decade.

New Zealand's remote location makes it seem far removed from the craziness of other parts of the world. That remoteness also means that it's a long flight to almost anywhere.

If you feel that you can afford to live in New Zealand, you need to allocate some additional money to invest there. An investment visa is the only way a retired person is going to qualify to reside there.

New Zealand offers a two-year temporary retirement visa which requires an investment of NZ $750,000 and an additional NZ $500,000 in funds to live on and an annual income of NZ $60,000 per year. You must be at least 66 years old. You can bring your spouse or partner, but not dependent children.

You must maintain your own health insurance and you cannot work on this visa. You can re-apply for another temporary retirement visa if you still meet all the conditions and can demonstrate that you have maintained your insurance and your investments during your 2-year stay.

PART NINE

LGBT Concerns

Chapter 37

Evaluating LGBT Resources and Friendliness

Lesbian, Gay, Bisexual, and Transgender (LGBT) people who are planning to move after they retire have all of the same concerns that have been covered throughout this book, plus an added layer. LGBT people need to ensure that the place they choose to live will be safe, offer legal protections and LGBT social and support organizations, and have open-minded and accepting people. It's important that a community offers LGBT-owned and LGBT-friendly businesses and services, particularly where medical and senior care facilities and services are concerned.

This section of the book will discuss the additional factors that LGBT people should consider when evaluating potential places to retire. It will suggest some places that are particularly welcoming, both in the United States and abroad. Some helpful resources will be mentioned here and linked on RetireFabulously.com/quest-resources.

For non-LGBT readers, a city's and country's acceptance of its LGBT citizens serves as a good indicator of how accepting it will be for people of all diverse demographics, such as ethnic minorities or religious minorities. Areas with rich diversity tend to offer more culinary choices and broader cultural offerings than areas with more homogenous populations.

Fortunately, acceptance of LGBT people has increased significantly in just the past decade. In the 2004, 2006, and 2008 elections, many states voted to enact state constitutional amendments which denied LGBT citizens equal marriage rights. There was still vocal opposition to allowing LGBT people to serve openly in the military.

During that era, it was easier to differentiate welcoming places to live from those that were unwelcoming on the basis of state and local laws on equal marriage, protection from employment discrimination, and other factors.

Now, the playing field is more level. The arrival of equal marriage and open service brought a remarkable shift in public opinion. According to a 2017 Gallop poll, 67 percent of Americans now support same-sex marriage. According to Pew Research Center,[27] in 2004, 60 percent of Americans opposed same-sex marriage, but in 2017, 62 percent supported it. Other polls offer similar statistics. Americans overwhelmingly support equal employment rights for LGBT people.

That makes it easier for LGBT people to live openly and comfortably in more places in the United States than ever before. We are getting closer to the day when LGBT people can choose their ideal retirement destination based on all the other factors mentioned in this book without having to be concerned with safety and acceptance. But we're not there yet.

And just as most states are not homogenous in many other regards, neither are states uniform with regard to acceptance (or not) of LGBT people. There are some excellent retirement options for LGBT people in red states and some areas of blue states that are best avoided.

The next chapter will profile the LGBT retirement communities that exist in the US, ranging from a beautiful, full-featured Continuing Care Retirement Community (CCRC) to LGBT-centric residential developments to government-subsidized low-income apartments.

Just like there are Best Places to Retire lists for the population at large, there are Best Places to Retire lists for LGBT living and retirement. All the same pros and cons apply when considering places on these lists. That said, most of the lists are pretty good. I will highlight

---

[27] https://www.pewforum.org/fact-sheet/changing-attitudes-on-gay-marriage/

some of the better places around the US and around the world in subsequent chapters.

There are several good resources for determining how LGBT-friendly a city or town is, and how well a destination you are considering will serve your needs.

The Human Rights Campaign (HRC), one of the oldest and most prominent LGBT advocacy organizations in the US, offers two detailed studies that are updated each year.

The first is the HRC Municipal Equality Index (MEI).[28] This index rates cities of all sizes in terms of how inclusive municipal laws, policies, and services are for LGBT people who live and work there. It includes factors such as laws which prevent discrimination, municipal employment policies, diversity training, services offered, and so on. The 2018 report rated 506 cities, of which 78 earned a perfect score of 100. Many more scored in the 80s and 90s. Some of the cities that scored 100 will surprise you, including such unlikely cities as Birmingham, Alabama; Brookings, South Dakota; Missoula, Montana; and Allentown, Pennsylvania.

It is encouraging to see the dramatic improvement of scores from year to year.

To be clear, this report measures the presence of inclusive municipal laws, policies, and services for LGBT people. It does not measure how accepting of LGBT people the local residents are or how comfortable *you* will feel living there. The latter would be difficult to measure objectively, but if you could, I think these two measurements would correlate closely. If the leadership of a city or town is progressive enough to enact legislation, implement policies, and provide services that are supportive of LGBT people, that should be a reflection of what the community wants.

The second is the HRC Healthcare Equality Index (HEI).[29] This index rates hospitals and other healthcare facilities on non-discrimination and staff training, patient services and support, employee benefits and policies, and patient and community engagement.

The 2019 report rated 680 facilities. This is by no means all of the hospitals in the country. Only hospitals that voluntarily submit their data are included in the report. But as with the MEI, the level of participation

---

[28] https://www.hrc.org/mei
[29] https://www.hrc.org/hei

increases each year, and the commitment of these facilities to LGBT inclusion increases considerably each year.

As you get older, you're going to need more medical care. Someday, you may have to move into an independent or assisted living facility or a nursing home. It helps to know whether there are supportive providers and facilities in places you are considering.

Services & Advocacy for GLBT Elders (SAGE) has created an excellent LGBT competency training program for senior service agencies and residential homes. Their website provides a searchable list of senior care providers[30] that have completed this LGBT competency training.

The Gay & Lesbian Medical Association (GLMA)[31] provides a directory of doctors and other medical service providers so you can determine the presence of LGBT doctors in a place you are considering.

Progress seems to be slowest when it comes to independent and assisted living and nursing facilities. Despite SAGE's valiant efforts, few facilities have completed SAGE's training program.

There are several websites which serve as nationwide directories of senior living facilities. They offer numerous search and filtering criteria, but none of them offer a search for LGBT inclusiveness. However, there are four ways you can assess whether there are LGBT-friendly retirement homes in your area.

First, the SAGE directory of senior service agencies lists, among other things, agencies that help people find senior living facilities in their area. They are sort of like the travel agents of the senior living industry. Since these agencies have completed the SAGE training, they should be able to point you to facilities in your area that would be good places to live.

Many medium and large cities in the US and Canada have Prime Timers clubs.[32] If there is a club in the area you are considering moving to, you can contact them and ask about LGBT-friendly senior homes in the area, as well as more general questions about whether the community is a good place to live for LGBT people. Prime Timers is a men's organization, but they would probably be willing to provide information to any LGBT person.

---

[30] https://sageusa.care/sagecare-providers/
[31] http://www.glma.org/
[32] https://www.primetimersww.com/

The LGBT community centers in many cities offer outreach specifically to older members of the community. Contact the local center and see if they can offer you information about services and facilities, as well as community information in general.

Most important, ask! Call facilities in your area, or better yet, visit. Ask if they welcome LGBT people. Ask if they have openly LGBT residents. Ask if their policies and training programs include sexual orientation and gender identity. Ask to see their non-discrimination policy, and ask how they handle discrimination complaints.

In some cases, you may be the first person or couple who has ever asked. The Washington Post reported on a 90-year-old man who approached the Asbury Methodist Village in Gaithersburg, MD about whether he and his same-sex partner would be welcome there. They couldn't offer any definitive information, but that prompted Asbury to take steps to become more welcoming to LGBT residents. In 2018, Asbury became the first facility in the Washington region to receive LGBT-friendly certification from SAGECare[33] – all because someone asked.

As time passes, more and more cities and medical service providers will become more competent at serving LGBT people. Even despite political fluctuations, progress towards equality continues and it is unlikely to regress.

---

[33] https://www.washingtonpost.com/local/social-issues/retirement-communities-turn-their-sights-on-a-once-invisible-group-lgbt-seniors/2018/07/08/3321c976-815a-11e8-b9a5-7e1c013f8c33_story.html

Chapter 38

Retirement Communities for LGBT Seniors

The Baby Boomer generation (those born between 1946 and 1964) is now retiring. According to SAGE, there are currently between 1.75 million and 4 million gays and lesbians over age 65. By 2030, that number is expected to nearly double.

Given these statistics, it seems reasonable to assume there could be a boom in the need for LGBT retirement community options. Over the past fifteen years, many projects have started, but most never made it out of the planning stages. The recession and real estate bust that occurred in the late 2000s scuttled some projects. But the question still remains: how big is the need for LGBT-focused retirement communities, now and in the future?

When I polled readers of RetireFabulously.com in August, 2013, 30 percent of the respondents said they would seriously consider living in an LGBT retirement community, and 50 percent said they might consider it if the community was located in the area they were planning to move to anyway.

Before we continue, it's important to distinguish between retirement homes and retirement communities. For the purposes of discussion in this book, a retirement home is a facility in which seniors require some level of assistance, from assisted living to full nursing home care. In these facilities, residents live in rooms or small suites. Conversely, retirement communities are those in which people maintain their own residence – either a detached home, mobile home, condo, or apartment. In the former, residents require some level of medical care or basic living support; in the latter, residents can live independently or with minimal assistance.

The need for LGBT-friendly retirement homes seems clear. For years, LGBT retirees suffered inhumane indignities during their final stages of life. The loneliness and isolation that accompany aging were often compounded by discrimination. For example, same-sex partners were denied the opportunity to share the same room. Staff members who personally object to homosexuality have treated LGBT elders insensitively. Finances and benefits normally given to heterosexual partners have been withheld from surviving same-sex partners. Many seniors had to go back into the closet when they entered the senior care system. While the situation has improved in recent years, far too many areas of the country are still backward and intolerant in this regard.

In a 2013 study conducted by the Equal Rights Center in Washington, DC, callers posing as same-sex couples and as opposite-sex couples contacted retirement homes in ten states. In 48 percent of the 200 tests across the ten states, the same-sex couples were offered information that was less favorable than what was offered to opposite-sex couples. Examples of this discrimination included being quoted different rates for rents, deposits, and fees, or opposite-sex testers being told about the availability of more units than same-sex testers were told about. The same-sex testers were also offered fewer incentives to rent and were presented with more application requirements or were steered away from the units they had requested, even though members of this group presented a slightly better financial profile than the heterosexual callers to the same facility.[34]

To me, the need for LGBT retirement communities (for independent and active retirees) is less compelling. As discussed earlier in this book, changing demographic trends across generations suggest that demand for age-segregated communities, many of which are on the outskirts or cities or in remote locations, will decline. I see more people choosing to stay in the mainstream of society. This especially applies to LGBT

---

[34] https://equalrightscenter.org/news-posts/opening-doors-an-investigation-of-barriers-to-senior-housing-for-same-sex-couples/

people, many of whom will want to remain connected to the LGBT community.

Personally, I don't want to live in a community that is exclusively senior, and I don't want to live in a community that is exclusively LGBT, either.

As Baby Boomers continue to age and retire, perhaps the market for LGBT retirement communities will grow as well. So far, that's not happening. But as the nation's acceptance of LGBT people continues to grow, the need and demand for these types of communities will more likely diminish.

I think our ultimate goal should be full inclusion into society, not more LGBT-centric communities where we live in a silo.

But that's just me. If you would prefer to live in an LGBT-exclusive community, you are entitled to that choice.

Here are the LGBT-focused retirement communities and homes that are currently operating in the United States. Links to these communities may be found at RetireFabulously.com/quest-resources. If new communities appear, I will add them to the website.

Fountaingrove Lodge in Santa Rosa, California, is a luxurious, full-featured LGBT retirement home. It's also the only LGBT Continuing Care Retirement Community (CCRC), meaning that you can move in being fully active and independent, then age in place as you require more levels of assistance. It's a bit pricey, but so are most CCRCs – and you get a lot of amenities and luxury for your money.

Seashore Point in Provincetown, Massachusetts, offers studio, one-bedroom, and two-bedroom condominium units for independent living. There's a wellness center on site. Should health needs arise, you can avail yourself of home health or companion services in your home, or take advantage of the professional rehab department.

Both Fountaingrove Lodge and Seashore Point offer a full schedule of activities, fitness center, restaurant-style dining, maintenance, and housekeeping.

Rainbow Vista in Gresham, Oregon, offers studio and one-bedroom apartments for independent living. They provide no medical or assisted living services. Communal facilities include a large event space, a comfortable area for chats, a video theater with large screen TV and surround sound, an exercise room, a game room with a pool table, and a music room.

A Place for Us in Cleveland, Ohio, offers one- and two-bedroom apartments. Amenities include a fitness center, meditation room, laundry facilities on every floor, and a library.

If you are active and independent, you have several options for owning your own home in an LGBT-centric residential development.

The Palms of Manasota in Palmetto, Florida, is the oldest and best-known LGBT retirement community in the United States, located between Sarasota and St. Petersburg. It was launched in 1994, and residents began moving in in 1998. The community filed for bankruptcy in October, 2011. Their website disappeared for a while but is now active again.

Carefree Cove in Boone, North Carolina, is an LGBT residential community in a mountain setting. The development features log cabin-style homes and still has one available lot as well as several resale homes.

Birds of a Feather is a gated LGBT community in a rural, mountainous setting near Pecos, New Mexico, about a half hour east of Santa Fe. Lots are still available.

The Resort on Carefree Boulevard in Fort Meyers, Florida, is a women-only community of manufactured homes and recreational vehicles (RVs).

Discovery Bay Resort is a small women-only development featuring small manufactured homes of about 400 sq. ft. (also known as Park Models) and RVs. It's located on the North Olympic Peninsula, about halfway between Sequim and Port Townsend, Washington.

The Pueblo is a women-only mobile home and RV park in Apache Junction, Arizona. They don't have a website, but they do have a Facebook group.

Stonewall Gardens in Palm Springs, California is the nation's first and only assisted living facility for LGBT seniors. Stonewall Gardens offers an on-site nurse, meals, and a 24-hour staff that assists with daily living needs such as medication management, dressing, grooming, bathing, and personal assistance.

In recent years, low-income retirement apartments created specifically for LGBT seniors have opened in several major cities. These facilities are government-subsidized and require low income qualifications for entry. In most cases, rent is calculated on a sliding scale based on about 30 percent of the renter's income. Affordable facilities are in high demand, and most of these were filled via a lottery system prior to opening. They remain fully occupied and their waiting lists are lengthy or closed. The demand clearly exceeds supply.

- Triangle Square, West Hollywood, California
- Spirit on Lake, Minneapolis, Minnesota
- John C. Anderson Apartments, Philadelphia, Pennsylvania
- Town Hall, Chicago, Illinois
- 55 Laguna, San Francisco, California (waitlist closed)
- North Park Senior Apartments, San Diego, California (waitlist closed)
- Ingersoll Senior Residences, New York City, New York

These low-income LGBT residential facilities are in the planning stages or under construction:

- Mary's House for Older Adults, Washington, DC
- Crotona Senior Residences, New York City, New York
- Village Hearth Cohousing, Durham, North Carolina
- The Residences at Equality Park, Wilton Manors, Florida

Until the day comes when LGBT seniors can fully avail themselves of all of the options available to other seniors without fear of being ostracized or discriminated against, it's good to know that these options exist.

Information in this chapter was current as of October, 2019. Please visit RetireFabulously.com/quest-resources periodically for updated information.

Chapter 39

Best US Cities for LGBT Retirees

When it comes to choosing a place to live during retirement, LGBT people want the same things that everyone else wants – safety, reasonable prices, agreeable climate, cultural and recreational amenities, and good healthcare.

However, LGBT people have a few additional factors to consider. Those include how tolerant an area is, the presence of a gay community, and healthcare providers that are welcoming towards LGBT people. Sadly, instances where LGBT patients are treated poorly and same-sex partners are denied visitation rights or decision-making rights in hospitals and nursing homes are still all too common.

In addition to considerations such as low cost of living and low taxes, LGBT people tend to value cities with strong LGBT communities, higher levels of acceptance, and the presence of non-discrimination laws.

Cities famous for their prominent LGBT communities, such as New York City, San Francisco, Los Angeles, and Washington, DC are also very expensive.

In the not-too-distant past, there weren't many other places that could be considered LGBT-friendly. Most places where everyone else flocked for retirement were definitely not places where LGBT people could live openly and comfortably.

Today, a substantial majority of Americans support marriage equality, open military service, and employment non-discrimination. There will always be intolerant folks, but their numbers continue to decline.

What that means for LGBT people is there is a much broader range of choices for where to live. In researching the LGBT friendliness of communities all over the country, I have learned that most cities (even smaller ones) have pride festivals, LGBT film festivals, and other hallmarks of an LGBT community.

Some age-restricted 55+ communities now have officially chartered LGBT clubs, along with dozens or even hundreds of other such affinity groups. Sun City, Sun City West, Sun City Grand, and Green Valley, all in Arizona, and The Villages in Florida have such chartered clubs. Most retirement communities in the Southeast have been slower to implement these.

Here are some cities that offer an excellent combination of affordability, culture, community, and LGBT friendliness that you may wish to consider. They are presented in no particular order.

Austin, Texas

Austin is a diverse, liberal oasis in an otherwise politically conservative state. However, it's worth noting that Dallas, Fort Worth, and San Antonio all scored 100 on the latest MEI ratings and have significant LGBT communities.

The city is home to the state government, the University of Texas, and many high-tech and pharmaceutical companies. Austin is famous for its live music scene, with more music venues per capita than any other US city. Austin is one of the most rapidly growing cities in the country, but many residents hope to preserve the city's quirky and artsy culture with the motto, "Keep Austin Weird." Winters are mild, but summers are very hot and often humid. According to a recent Gallup poll, Austin has the third-largest percentage of LGBT residents in the country.

Atlanta, Georgia

Most areas of the Deep South aren't particularly welcoming of LGBT people, but Atlanta and neighboring DeKalb County offer a cosmopolitan environment with plenty of art, music, and culture. There's a bustling bar and restaurant scene and community groups for all interests. Several neighborhoods, such as Midtown and Avondale Estates, have numerous businesses that serve the LGBT community. And if your retirement plans include travel, the huge Hartsfield-Jackson airport offers direct flights to hundreds of domestic and international destinations.

Phoenix, Arizona

Arizona has a reputation of being politically conservative, but the state has now moved to the center. Most areas of Phoenix are quite welcoming of LGBT people. The Valley of the Sun's plentiful 55+ active adult communities are located around the outskirts of town, but LGBT retirees will probably prefer some of Phoenix's well-preserved historic neighborhoods or the nearby suburbs of Tempe, Chandler, or Ahwatukee. Phoenix has grown rapidly over the past several decades, and so has its gay community, foodie scene, and cultural options. Winters are delightful, but you'll want to have access to a pool to enjoy the hot summers.

Tucson, Arizona

If the Phoenix metro area is too large and spread out for your tastes, consider Tucson. This metro area of 700,000 has plenty of arts and culture thanks to the University of Arizona, a somewhat slower pace, and beautiful mountains on all four sides. Tucson, and much of southern Arizona, is more liberal than most other areas in the state.

Orlando, Florida

This central Florida city may be best known for Disney World, Universal Studios, Sea World, and other tourist attractions, but there is much more to Orlando than just its theme parks. Orlando has a well-established gay community and several popular gentrified neighborhoods such as Thornton Park, Lake Eola Heights, and Colonialtown. The cost of living, house prices and tax rates are particularly low in Orlando. And if you are hoping that many of your friends will visit after you retire, the proximity to the ubiquitous theme parks can't hurt.

Tampa and St. Petersburg, Florida

When you think of popular gay destinations in Florida, Fort Lauderdale, Wilton Manors, and Key West are usually the first cities that come to mind. But they're expensive. Tampa and nearby St. Petersburg offer larger-city amenities at a much lower cost. The Ybor City neighborhood in Tampa, a National Historic Landmark District, is growing as a gay neighborhood. South Tampa hosts the Tampa Pride festival and is home to numerous LGBT venues and businesses. St. Petersburg hosts the largest LGBT pride festival in the state as well as world-class museums and a growing art scene.

Columbus, Ohio

Home to one of the largest universities in the country and numerous corporate headquarters, Columbus is well-educated, open-minded, cultured, and definitely LGBT-friendly. German Village, just south of downtown, is quaint neighborhood that is popular with gays and lesbians, while the Short North area just north of downtown is home to numerous galleries. Columbus has a thriving jazz scene, and there are plenty of music and theatre performances offered at Ohio State and downtown. The winters can be harsh, but the low cost of living and real estate make the area easily affordable.

Salt Lake City, Utah

It may seem surprising that the same city that is home to the world headquarters of the Mormon Church is also home to the seventh largest per-capita LGBT population in the US, according to a recent Gallup poll. But Salt Lake City, which elected a lesbian mayor in 2016, is an island of liberal, progressive thinking with a thriving gay community. Winters are cold, but there is world-class skiing nearby as well as the famous Sundance Film Festival in nearby Park City.

Dallas, Texas

For many years, Dallas has had a strong, vibrant LGBT community centered around the Oak Lawn neighborhood and, more recently, the Bishop Arts District. The Turtle Creek Chorale has been one of the country's best-regarded men's choruses for decades. Dallas is home to the Cathedral of Hope, the largest LGBT church in the world. The cost of living, house prices, and taxes are all relatively affordable in Dallas.

Denver, Colorado

The Denver area is home to the nation's ninth largest per-capita LGBT population, as well as a thriving LGBT and cultural scene. If you enjoy the mountains for hiking, skiing, or breath-taking beauty, the Denver area is hard to beat. Since real estate in Denver itself is a bit pricey, you may wish to consider nearby Aurora, where the cost of living is slightly lower and the median house price is significantly less than in Denver.

Portland, Oregon / Vancouver, Washington

In the past couple decades, Portland, Oregon has become one of the trendiest destinations in the US, both for the Millennial generation and for the LGBT community, which is the second-largest per-capita in the country. Portland has mild winters and beautiful summers, but it's rainy throughout most of the year. Portland also has expensive real estate and Oregon has a relatively high tax burden, so a more economical option would be to settle across the Columbia River in Vancouver, Washington, where the median house price is significantly lower. This option allows you to live in Washington, where there is no state income tax, and shop in Oregon, where there is no sales tax.

Pittsburgh, Pennsylvania

Pittsburgh has been working hard for the past couple decades to modernize and revitalize itself as a great place to live, and the results are starting to show. While still not a gay mecca (its MEI is score 90 but it suffers with regard to LGBT-friendly hospitals), it scores better than average in cost of living, real estate, healthcare, and crime rate.

Las Vegas, Nevada

Las Vegas has the lowest MEI score of these cities, with a still-respectable 87. Cost of housing is average, but all other metrics are good. Las Vegas offers lots of sunshine and warm temperatures in a desert environment very similar to Phoenix. Las Vegas isn't for everyone, but if the retirement lifestyle you desire includes lots of entertainment and shows, this may be the place. Las Vegas has several nice suburbs to the south.

Most lists of top retirement destinations focus on medium to large cities. For LGBT retirees, as well as many others who prefer places with diverse populations with thriving arts and culture scenes, larger cities usually have the most to offer. Larger cities also provide more options for medical care and senior support services.

But if you prefer the more relaxed pace of small town living but still hope to find an inclusive and welcoming community with a fun, artsy ambiance, you're in luck. Here are several smaller LGBT-friendly towns with big personalities that are worth your consideration as retirement destinations.

Asheville, North Carolina

Asheville is artsy, progressive, scenic, and it is one of the most gay-friendly cities in the southeast. If you love the mountains and milder weather, Asheville is worth a look.

Bloomington, Indiana

Bloomington scores a perfect 100 on the MEI, and Indiana University offers many cultural opportunities. It has a good gay community with an annual Pridefest and an LGBT film festival. The surrounding area is beautiful, with mountains, forests, lakes, and the large Brown County State park for outdoor recreation.

Madison, Wisconsin

Madison was the #1 retirement city in the Milken Institute's extensive Best Cities for Successful Aging report. It scored 100 on the MEI, is highly rated for healthcare, but gets very cold in winter.

Northampton, Massachusetts

This town in western Massachusetts was once dubbed "Lesbianville, USA" by the National Enquirer, because it has long been a welcoming, inclusive place for LGBT people. The area has a thriving creative community with arts and film festivals throughout the year.

Walla Walla, Washington

Walla Walla offers an LGBT-friendly, welcoming college-town vibe. The Walla Walla Valley is famous for its many vineyards, and there are about a dozen small breweries and distilleries in the area. The weather is sunny and dry, and there are beautiful mountains nearby.

Eugene and Corvallis, Oregon

Eugene and Corvallis, home to Oregon's two largest universities, offer a smaller and more affordable option to Portland.

Bisbee, Arizona

During its copper mining heyday in the early 1900s, Bisbee was the largest city between St. Louis and San Francisco. Today this town of 5,575 in the southeast corner of Arizona has transformed into a vibrant, quirky town with interesting shops, a thriving arts and music scene, and remarkably well-preserved 1900-era architecture. There are dozens of unique local restaurant choices and western-style saloons. You'll see plenty of rainbow decals in the windows.

Real estate prices and overall cost of living are well below national averages, and temperatures are moderate year-round. When you need to venture to a larger city, Tucson is 80 miles to the northwest. Bisbee was voted 'America's Best Historic Small Town' by USA Today readers.

One downside to Bisbee is it's hilly. If you advance to the point where walking up steps or steep inclines is challenging, your ability to move about freely may become limited. Streets are narrow and parking is limited; Bisbee is definitely a walking town.

Saugatuck and Douglas, Michigan

The adjacent towns of Saugatuck and Douglas, on the shore of Lake Michigan, have a combined year-round population of about 2,000. But these towns can swell to three times that size during the summer season. Saugatuck's Oval Beach has been named one of the top 25 beaches in the world by Conde Nast and the nearby sand dunes are visually stunning. Between the two towns, there are over 140 LGBT-owned or friendly shops, galleries, restaurants and lodging options.

While Saugatuck and Douglas thrive during the summer months, winters are cold and annual snowfall is over six feet. Median house prices are approximately $300,000, which makes this area a more expensive choice. When you need a big city, Grand Rapids is just 40 miles away. It might make more sense to live in Grand Rapids and visit Saugatuck.

Yellow Springs, Ohio

This small, woody town of 3,500 about 20 miles east of Dayton earned its reputation as a liberal oasis during the hippie movement of the 1960s. Today, its small downtown is lined with shops, galleries, and a tiny long-standing art film theater, many of which sport rainbow flags and decals. Homes are inexpensive, the cost of living is low, and there's plenty of hiking to enjoy in nearby Glen Helen and John Bryan State Park. When you need big city amenities, Dayton is nearby and Columbus and Cincinnati are both about an hour away. Yellow Springs experiences typical Ohio winters with below-freezing temperatures and an average annual snowfall of over two feet.

Moab, Utah

Moab is a small, isolated town in eastern Utah, situated between the Arches and Canyonlands National Parks, both renowned for their stunning natural beauty. The area thrives on outdoor adventure and is popular with mountain bikers, hikers, and whitewater rafters. Downtown Moab offers an interesting array of restaurants, galleries, and shops. The town began to establish its reputation as an LGBT-welcoming place several years ago when over 500 of its 5,000 residents turned out to participate in Moab's first-ever Pride parade and festival. Now, the town stages annual events including A Day in the Park, the Visibility March, and Gay Adventure Week. House prices and cost of living are close to the national averages. Since Moab is situated in an arid high desert region, it experiences chilly winters and warm summers with light annual precipitation and snowfall.

However, Moab is remote. The nearest large city, Salt Lake City, is over 230 miles away.

It's worth noting that many of these cities (Phoenix/Tempe, Tucson, Austin, Columbus, Madison, Eugene, Corvallis, and Bloomington) are home to large universities, which offer cultural amenities and adult learning opportunities that are beneficial to retirees.

Chapter 40

LGBT Laws and Rights Around the World

The past two decades have brought great progress towards LGBT equality and more accepting attitudes towards LGBT people throughout western Europe, North and South America, New Zealand, and Australia. That's not as true in the Caribbean and parts of Central America, however, 2018 brought a couple landmark rulings.

In January 2018, the Inter-American Court of Human Rights (IACHR) declared that its signatory countries should legalize same-sex marriage.[35] The decision was issued in response to a petition from Costa Rica's president Luis Guillermo Solis, who supports equal rights for LGBT people in his country. Costa Rica will legalize same-sex marriage on May 26, 2020. Ecuador has recently enacted same-sex marriage as a result of this ruling.

The other countries that are supposedly bound by this ruling which have not yet legalized same-sex marriage are Barbados, Chile, El Salvador, Guatemala, Haiti, Nicaragua, Panama, Peru, and Suriname. Bolivia, the Dominican Republic, Honduras, and Paraguay are signatories to the IACHR but have constitutional bans on same-sex marriage.

---

[35] https://www.nbcnews.com/feature/nbc-out/latin-american-human-rights-court-urges-same-sex-marriage-legalization-n836386

Chile currently has civil unions.

Later in 2018, the European Court of Justice ruled that married same-sex couples have the same residency rights as married opposite-sex couples under EU law, even if same-sex marriage is not legal in that particular EU member state. The ruling affects all EU countries, which are obliged to abide by it, including possible retirement destinations Greece, Italy, and Croatia, which have civil unions.

In early 2019, Thailand passed a law to recognize same-sex couples as civil partners, with limited rights including being able to make medical decisions and own and inherit property. Thai society has long been permissive in larger cities and popular tourist areas. LGBT people have some legal protections.

Thailand is the only country in Asia that would be a good choice for LGBT people, in terms of legal protections. Taiwan recently became the first Asian country to legalize same-sex marriage, but it does not have a provision for retirement immigration.

Laws around the world are changing rapidly. Equaldex.com is an excellent resource for all LGBT rights by country, beyond just equal marriage rights.

In 2018, the Williams Institute at the UCLA School of Law released a report measuring LGBT Global Acceptance in 141 countries,[36] based on the combined data of 11 previous global surveys by various organizations.

The legalization of same-sex marriage is important not only for the benefits it accrues to same-sex couples, but it is an indicator of a country's overall acceptance of LGBT people. Plus, as immigrants, it makes it easier to get both spouses into a country.

As of October, 2019, these countries recognize same-sex marriages:

- The Netherlands (2000)
- Belgium (2003)
- Canada (2005)
- Spain (2005)*
- South Africa (2006)*
- Norway (2008)
- Sweden (2009)

---

[36] https://williamsinstitute.law.ucla.edu/research/lgbt-acceptance-inclusion-worldwide/

- Mexico (2009 – recognized nationwide, but not performed in every state)*
- Iceland (2010)
- Portugal (2010)*
- Argentina (2010)*
- Denmark (2012)
- Uruguay (2013)*
- New Zealand (2013)*
- France (2013)*
- Brazil (2013)*
- England and Wales (2013)
- Scotland (2014)
- Luxembourg (2014)
- Finland (2015)
- Ireland (2015)
- Greenland (2015)
- United States (2015)
- Colombia (2016)*
- Germany (2017)*
- Malta (2017)*
- Australia (2017)
- Austria (2019)*
- Taiwan (2019)
- Ecuador (2019)*
- Costa Rica (2020)*

* indicates a country where retirement immigration is possible.

It's been a remarkable 20 years!

Generally, the presence of same-sex marriage is a good barometer for the acceptance of homosexuality by the people of a country. Even so, you'll find more acceptance in the cities and less acceptance in rural areas.

One notable exception is South Africa. Although it was the fifth country to legalize same-sex marriage, it doesn't score well in the Williams 2018 ranking of LGBT acceptance in 141 countries mentioned above, scoring only 4.00 on their scale of 0-10. Cape Town has a vibrant

LGBT community, but most of the rest of the country is still largely homophobic.

Based on this data, all of the countries profiled earlier in this book would be good choices for LGBT people to immigrate to.

PART TEN

Conclusion

Chapter 41

Can Moving to the Right Place Really Make You Happier?

Well, yes and no.

As the old expression goes, money can't buy happiness. That's true, but a lack of money can certainly cause unhappiness. And beyond meeting basic needs, a sufficient amount of money will enable you to afford some of the items and activities that you will enjoy, bringing happiness.

Similarly, the place you live, by itself, will not make you happy. However, living in a place you dislike, for whatever reasons, can easily make you unhappy. You can satisfy your basic needs almost anywhere, but choosing the best place to live will enable you enjoy the activities and people that will make your retirement satisfying.

In my first book, *Design Your Dream Retirement: How to Envision, Plan For, and Enjoy the Best Retirement Possible*, I asserted that in order to enjoy a happy retirement, you need to curate your life with a balance of physical activity, mental stimulation, socialization, and fulfillment. If you choose a place that provides the things you want across these four categories, then living in that place will enable your happiness.

Chapter 42

Are You Ready to Embark Upon Your Quest?

Throughout this book, I have attempted to share everything I have learned about finding and moving to the place where you will best be able to enjoy your retirement – in other words, your Retirement Utopia.

At times, it may seem like the information I presented was more negative than positive, as if I was trying to talk you out of moving after you retire. That's not the case at all. My goal is to enable you to make the most informed, well-reasoned decision possible.

One of my biggest complaints about many websites and books that deal with moving after you retire is that they often paint an unrealistically rosy picture of potential retirement destinations. This is particularly true with some websites that encourage moving overseas.

My intention is not for the negative to outweigh the positive. It is to provide a more realistic balance when you consider the information in this book along with the information you read in other places. I would rather show you the potential obstacles and have you work through them than to leave them unaddressed only to become an unpleasant surprise after you move.

I have made two major moves in my life – one from Ohio to the Washington, DC area and one from the DC area to Arizona. Both of those moves resulted in major leaps forward in almost every aspect of my life, including new opportunities, career and personal growth, new friends, and new things to discover. Each move was an adventure.

I choose to view retirement as an adventure, and I hope you will too. Moving, if done purposefully, can be an immensely rewarding part of this adventure. Moving can place you in the best position, literally, to enjoy your retirement to its fullest.

The quest for Retirement Utopia is not just a quest for the most beautiful or most economically advantageous place, it's a quest for an optimal, wonderful life. I wish you nothing but happiness and success in your quest!

Gratitude

I would like to express my sincere gratitude to:

Cathy and Jeff Lincourt, Mark McNease and Frank Murray, Paula Coffer, Terry Henning and Brian Worley, and Rob Teichman and Roy Bickford, who contributed their stories of moving after they retired. Their stories added personality, interest, and invaluable first-hand experience to this book.

Debra Gaskill, for her excellent input as editor of this book. Debra, a friend of mine from high school, is a career journalist, newspaper editor, and author of a series of mystery novels. Please visit DebraGaskillNovels.com to discover Debra's work.

Mark McNease, for his unwavering support, encouragement, and great advice. Mark is a successful author of mystery novels and anthologies. He did an excellent job as the editor of my first two books. Please visit MarkMcNease.com to discover Mark's work.

Alejandro Jimenez, for his recommendations for where to live in Costa Rica.

Paul Fox, for his enthusiastic support and encouragement, and for bringing me to Pittsburgh, Pennsylvania to present my workshop.

Linda Abels, founder of Abels Financial Services, for bringing me to Forest City, Iowa to present my workshop.

John Brady, founder, writer, and administrator of TopRetirements.com, for creating such a thorough and useful body of work.

Everyone who subscribes to the *Retire Fabulously!* website or follows the *Retire Fabulously!* page on Facebook. Many of my readers have provided thoughtful comments and participated in surveys which informed the content of this book. You make doing all of this worthwhile.

Most of all, my husband, Jeff McKeehan, for his constant support, his valuable feedback, and his efforts to help promote *Retire Fabulously!* Jeff endures, without complaint, the long hours I have spent working on my website and this book that I could have spent with him and our dog. Every spouse of a writer will understand exactly what I'm talking about.

About the Author

Dave Hughes is a leading authority on retirement lifestyle planning. He writes about retirement lifestyle planning on his website, RetireFabulously.com and in his previous books, *Design Your Dream Retirement: How to Envision, Plan For, and Enjoy the Best Retirement Possible* and *Smooth Sailing into Retirement: How to Navigate the Transition from Work to Leisure.*

In 2016-2017, Dave was a regular contributor to U.S. News' *On Retirement* blog. In 2017, RetireFabulously.com received the Best Senior Living Award from SeniorHomes.com as one of the top retirement blogs, by both reader polling and judge's selection. Dave was named one of NextAvenue.org's Top 50 Influencers in Aging for 2017.

Following a successful 34-year career as a software engineer, trainer and course developer, and manager, Dave accepted an early retirement package and retired at age 56.

During the final phase of his working career Dave started searching the Internet for information about what life in retirement is really like. He discovered that at least 95% of all the retirement-related information was focused on the financial aspects of retirement – how much money you'll need, how you should shift your investment mix as you get older, how fast you can draw down your savings, and so on. Relatively little was being written about how to live a happy, fulfilling life during retirement, and of that, practically nothing was being written from an LGBT perspective.

Dave created RetireFabulously.com to fill that void. Dave has extensively researched retirement lifestyle issues, as well as drawing upon his own experiences of transitioning into retirement and those of others.

Dave is an accomplished public speaker and workshop leader. He was active in Toastmasters International for over eight years, and has earned Distinguished Toastmaster, that organization's highest honor. Dave offers a fun and engaging workshop, also called Retire Fabulously!, that brings to life many of the key messages that he presents on his website and in this book.

In addition to writing articles for RetireFabulously.com and books about retirement lifestyle planning, Dave is jazz musician who plays trombone, electric bass, and steel pan. Dave lives in the suburbs of Phoenix, Arizona with his husband Jeff and their dog Maynard.

Dave is available for interviews, speaking engagements, workshops, panel discussions, and writing guest articles. You may contact Dave at TQFRU-book@retirefabulously.com.

Please visit these websites to learn more:

RetireFabulously.com

TheDaveHughes.com

Made in the USA
San Bernardino, CA
04 January 2020